NKAR

The Village of Myths and Legends

Fr. Eugen Nkardzedze

En Route Books and Media, LLC

St. Louis, MO

⎈ENROUTE
Make the time

En Route Books and Media, LLC
5705 Rhodes Avenue
St. Louis, MO 63109

Cover credit: Eugen Nkardzedze

ISBN-13: 979-8-88870-044-0
Library of Congress Control Number: available at
https://catalog.loc.gov/

TABLE OF CONTENTS

PREFACE

My childhood and young adulthood were all spent in Nkar village, making me one of those whom you can take out of Nkar, but you cannot take Nkar out of them. I cannot think of a better way anyone could have expressed the attraction that this ancient village holds for many of us like a spell than to tell the story of its myths and legends as Fr Eugen Nkardzedze has done in this priceless book entitled *Nkar: The Village of Myths and Legends* with gratifying accounts of the priests who harnessed the devil in a bottle and a classical interview on the conversion of Wuber, the legendary thief. This book has vindicated great justice to the history, culture, religion, and the general anthropology of the great people of my village. The author has told the stories with the valour of humour and literature that seems to flow so effortlessly in his Nkar blood. It is an honour for those who will have this book on the menu of their literary dinner.

Mbuwir Irinus Sahfe aka Taankar

INTRODUCTION

"Behind every myth lies a truth; beyond every legend is reality, as radiant (sometimes as chilling) as the story itself." This assertion couldn't be truer in Nkar Village, where myth and reality get so intermingled, that it can take the genius to see the obvious. As one of the oldest settlements on the Bamenda-Kumbo Highway, *Mile 55* is always identified with Nkar village. A very self-contained village with hundreds of years in one and the same location, what would really make someone want to leave Nkar for somewhere else? There is no place like Nkar, a micro world bestowed with everything possible. If you are looking for someone or something, come to Nkar, the village of myths and legends, where even cats move around with the dignity of a-newly-returned-from-London.

Instead of the hanging gardens, as was in Babylon, John Ninga'h of Taaron constructed but a hanging bed, which he operated with ropes. He could lower himself down to the floor by pulling the rope-buttons according to design. He didn't store water in containers like buckets, but had live water connected from a nearby stream to run through his house. The bed hung over this passing stream, which was not too far from the fireside. He would bring himself down for a drink, attend to his pot on fire, and then bring himself up again by pulling the ropes. Another ingenious architect was Joe Kaisar who built a toilet on the trees after he heard that a pig bit someone's buttocks in Foumbot. From that day, Joe constructed his toilet on a tree where he did his hygienic business until one night he fell and injured his leg very badly.

Customarily, Nkar people do not tell lies; they only exaggerate things, like Baa Mborong who shot thirty-seven birds with one stone. The reality is that he shot a bird. Or Roland Njonsai who waited for thirty minutes while a snake crossed the road. To verify if it was still crossing, he harvested some leaves and threw them over the snake, and the leaves moved into the bush, a sign that the snake was still crossing, which means, it must have been so many miles long. He said, the snake is known as *dãwong*, meaning "across the world." The bottom line is that Roland

Njonsai saw a very long snake. This exaggeration syndrome may also explain why the village is full of storytellers who can hold you spellbound with tales that grow tails, until your pot gets burned on the fire. They can multiply loaves of bread and fish that can feed thousands of people, including women and children, and still collect twelve basketfuls of leftovers. Fr. Cornelius Sa'fe is also from Nkar and can bear testimony to this. He can even explain better. And Fr Andrew Ngah accepts that his explanations are true.

Nkar Village could conveniently run a school of exaggerations and fabulous tales with men and women who can describe River Tsemkan, the mainstream in the village that sometimes dwindles to a mere trickle in the dry season and even dries up completely when the season is harsh; they would refer to it as the mighty Tsemkan, making you think it was the forgotten Mississippi of Africa.

Besides providing water for various domestic uses in the village, Shey Taa, Oya, and Wanpep can testify with gratitude how the Tsemkan once rescued them from a hygienic situation that could have become a public embarrassment. These three friends had developed the bad habit of warming themselves with urine anytime they were caught in rain; they would just let it flow unto their pants. After all, it was raining, and they were already wet. It gave them some momentary warmth. Well, ninety-nine days for the thief and one day for the master. On this fateful day, they were very sure of a downpour that was making its way from the front towards them, as they carried some firewood on their heads, heading home from the farm. They were ready to be soaked, and decided to anticipate the urine-warming when the rain was still some distance away. Unfortunately, the rain literally jumped over their heads and continued falling behind and away from them. They felt like chasing after it, but there was really nothing they could do to make the rain fall on them. Thank God for River Tsemkan into which they graciously immersed themselves and neutralized the situation before they were able to reach home without looking funny and out of place. It is never advisable to take anything in Nkar at face value, even the rains.

In his recently published book: *From the Highlands of Nkar to the World*, Martin Jumbam recalls the following about teachers in Nkar:

> They turned out to be much more than just class teachers; they were also community leaders to whom many people relied for advice. Many of them had been trained in Catholic teacher training colleges either within the British Southern Cameroons territory, or in neighbouring Nigeria. What was also remarkable about them was their unflinching devotion to duty. Teaching was not a job for them, it was a vocation which they accomplished to the best of their ability.[1]

If the village teachers went two miles when asked to go one, then nothing short of more should be expected of those who passed through their hands.

They were resilient and persevering. They were taught never to let the fish off the hook simply

---

[1] Martin Jumbam, *From the Highlands of Nkar to the World* (Denver, Colorado: Spears Books, 2022), 37-38.

because it bit their little finger, like the little boy in the old nursery rhyme:

> One, two, three, four, five.
> Once I caught a fish alive.
> Six, seven, eight, nine, ten.
> Then I let it go again.
> Why did you let it go?
> Because it bit my finger so.
> Which finger did it bite?
> This little finger on the right.

Basic education was considered as the base for everything in Nkar. It was the liberal cultivation of the entire person, as the school taught everything from hard work to handwriting. And that did not go without its own myths and legends, as the friends of Anthony Mbuwir of Mamfe compound believed his handwriting was so neat that it even resembled the handwriting on the Tablets of the Decalogue received from God by Moses on Mount Sinai.

In St. Mary's School Nkar, there were legendry teachers like Anthony Tala, known in his days as

Chia Baa. This was out of respect for his longevity in the profession and the fatherly manner with which he handled his everlasting class one. It used to feel as if the entire school building was shaking each time Chia Baa pronounced the letter "r". When it was lesson time for sounds and letters, the entire school was involved. From class one to class seven, no one could avoid hearing "rrrrrrrrrrrrrrrrrrrrrrrr" resounding down the block. Even parents passing on the road and those working in nearby farms came to learn the letter "r" without paying any fees, because of Chia Baa. In that way, it could be said that everyone in the village was taught by Chia Baa. Therefore, when it was Friday afternoon, the entire village joined in the chorus:

We come to school on Monday,
Tuesday, and Wednesday,
Thursday, and Friday,
It's time for us to go!

Goodbye to you teacher!
Goodbye to you teacher!

Goodbye to you teacher!
It's time for us to go.

St. Mary's School Nkar

Nkar the beautiful, where even the moon seems larger than elsewhere, and stars twinkle with extra acknowledgment, appearing earlier in the sky so as not to miss household stories when families would gather around the fireplaces for the evening tales. Streaks from the moon light filter through the tall kola nut trees of Kov Nkar, as a deserved quiet descends on the village with only Shey Ngai's voice harassing the silence. Nobody blames him, for sometimes he sings at night when he is frightened by the dark. However, that is when some people used to harvest kola nuts when it did not belong to them.

Tall as tall could be, there was no tree too tall for Roger Lahndze to climb. His rival was his cousin Rosemary Fondzebam. They were all youngsters from Mamfe compound. Fondzebam could climb trees so tall that those who saw her sitting on the branches could do nothing but beg her to come down gently. "*Kiiwo yaa. Kiiwo. Ku se'ey ji weh weh*," they pleaded. Roger had the pleasure of reaching to the highest point of the tree and harvesting the pods of kola nuts with his hands rather than with a stick. There was no tree he could not climb. He had an intimate relationship with kola nuts, and it was reputed that if you mixed kola nut pods from twenty different trees, he could sort and identify to which tree each of them belonged. That was possible, for we could also do the same, only to a lesser degree, for growing up in Kov Nkar meant having a connectivity with trees especially of kola nuts, oranges, pears, and coffee. You also learned how to make pears and bananas get ripe at the time you needed them, either by rubbing them underfoot or knowing where to place them and for how long. You also had to learn how to treat minor wounds and scratches with dust and other liquids. There were tree-climbing adventures that surviving to write about them can only be by the grace of God.

Everyone climbed trees in Kov Nkar, boys and girls alike, and you needed to be of very strong moral character to have grown up in Kov Nkar without stealing kola nuts. That could have been the background to Bishop Jules Peeters' anxiety, when he reportedly said in church that he would advise and redirect any young man he saw going behind the church, that is, going to Kov Nkar, to look for a wife. It had the cream of the headstrong boys and girls. What the Bishop did not know then was that a cross-section of priests and nuns from Nkar would hail from Kov Nkar.

You could not grow up in Kov Nkar without being tough, learning the language of the trees and the birds, and their names and manners. When one of the biggest kola nut trees, which was called *langi'*, fell due to age, there was sadness in Kov Nkar as if it was a person that had died. We used to spend time under that tree which was next to the legendry Yuwah tree from which our lineage family got its title name. We spent Sunday leisure time under its shade, learning kola nut lessons from our elder brothers while waiting for nuts to fall. Kola nuts were so important that they enjoyed special liberties compared to other nuts and fruits. You could pick kola nuts from under a pear or an orange tree, but pears and oranges that lay away from their mother trees were always suspected for not being good, somehow. But not the glorious precious kola nuts; if you picked any and looked up at the tree, it was only to verify if there was more up there, before running to Baa Lo'ti to sell. If he had no cash on him, we traded by barter. After all, no one really eats money. The bad side of trading by barter with Baa Lo'ti was that if you chose honey as your exchange payment, you could only dip your index finger into the jar once. If your hand was little and you did not know how to manipulate the dipping, then *ashia* for you.

Besides oranges, the sale of kola nuts constituted the most common source of income for children. If you were travelling on the Bamenda-Kumbo Highway and the bus stopped around Mile 55 and you saw children running towards it with buckets filled with oranges looking like balls of gold, and shouting: "Woren 50! Woren 50!" then you had reached Nkar, the village of myths and legends; the village of Doctor Leonard Sunjo whose healing touch became such a legend that many preferred it to medications. The way he attended to sick people and spoke to them with great understanding and care made even elderly sick people to walk long distances to Shisong Hospital, just to be touched by Doctor Sunjo from Nkar.

The Myths of Legends and the Legends of Myths

A dictionary definition of myth presents it as "a traditional story, especially one concerning the early history of a people or explaining some natural or social phenomenon, and typically involving supernatural beings or events." This makes it common for myth and legend to always appear together. People are generally protective of their myth, even when its facts do not tally with those of scientific reality. Accordingly, myth can be a great enemy of philosophy in that, while philosophy digs for the facts of reality in their deepest causes and reasons, myth offers improbable solutions to probable problems by covering them with old wives' tales that are designed to harness questions and stop children from being inquisitive. It provides answers that are not necessarily solutions, which only helps to postpone matters by offering excuses for not getting into the bushes and forests, climbing up hills and going down valleys to find out where a river takes its source and where it empties its waters. Where myth ends is where philosophy begins, for myth does not leave home. It has the tendency to sit on the branches while felling down the same tree.

Demythologization is therefore not always a welcome process among a people because it can puncture the balloons of their mindset. It entails saying that something they believe to be real is not real after all. It is the belief that creates the reality rather than reality creating the belief. R.C. Miller refers to this mindset as the theory of doublethink:

> *Doublethink* means the power of holding two contradictory beliefs simultaneously, and accepting both of them. The party intellectually knows that he is playing tricks with reality, but by the exercise of *doublethink* he also satisfies himself that reality is not violated.[2]

This resembles the mindset of sin; the sinner knows something to be morally wrong and yet goes on to do it while believing at the same time that what is wrong is somehow right or good. John Henry Newman refers to it as a form of madness. It is also the juju mindset represented by the mask; the people know that behind the mask is a human being, but they believe it to be a spirit at the same time, albeit a visible

---

[2] R.C. Miller, *The Language Gap and God: Religious Language and Christian Education* (Boston: Pilgrim Press, 1979), 24.

one. Therefore, unmasking a juju in public only presents questions whose answers nobody wants.

The episode in *The White Man of God* bespeaks the embarrassment of the people of Nkar when the priest unmasked the Kibarankoh, the big-headed juju, the blackest and most dangerous juju of the land, only to discover that the person behind the dreaded mask was the head catechist, Mathew. The juju had chosen the wrong time and place for its display and came around the churchyard at Benediction time, thus distracting everyone from going to church. The parish priest (Big Father) could not take it. Kenjo Jumbam, the celebrated storyteller from Nkar, narrates the incident of the abomination:

> Everybody held his breath as Big Father got closer to it and it had still not seen him. He gave it a kick on the bottom and everybody, especially the women, escaped into the bush and screamed. Did any of them see Big Father kick the biggest juju of the land? No nobody could see a thing like that because seeing it could mean a curse on him that saw it. One of the men in the juju group that

warns the public of approaching danger raised an alarm that darkness had fallen upon the tribe at midday and everybody should mind himself, for it was a man that ran away from danger and never danger from man. The alarm had the desired effect and everybody disappeared from sight in a moment. Even those who were in the open field ran into the bush and fell down and closed their eyes. Big Father kicked and kicked the *Kibarankoh* and when it turned round to him he pushed off its big mask and then got the shock of his life. Face to face with the juju he could not believe his eyes.

'Mathew!'
'Father.'
'Mathew!'
'Father.'

Then he collapsed on the spot. The juju put on his mask and ran back to the palace wilder

than ever. Did people witness this event? No, nobody did.[3]

The people considered it a moral responsibility to
protect the head of the *Kibarankoh* by choosing not
to know what they knew about it. One can therefore
understand why the people of Guinea in West Africa
did not take it in good faith when Camara Laye "took
off the mask" from the roaring lions by demystifying
the myth of their existence. In his novel *L'Enfant
Noir (African Child or The Dark Child)*, he describes
how, after taking part in the Kondén Diara nights
that served as the prelude to the circumcision of
young boys in his tribe, he learns that the frightful
roaring of the lions came but from the older boys and
not from lions really. Kondén Diara was a haunting
figure presented to children as master of lions, who
could drag anyone into the woods to devour. When
he roars, the frightful sound is resounded as by thirty
lions. For the boys to transit to manhood, they must
first spend a night in a cleared patch in the bush and

---

[3] Kenjoy Jumbam, *The White Man of God,* 143.

gain courage through overcoming their fears by confronting the roaring of Kondén Diara, then, they are circumcised. As he grew up, Laye discovered there was no Kondén Diara, but the older boys with instruments that produced roaring sounds like lions. He described the instruments as boards attached to strings that produce the sound when swung overhead. This simple tribal ritual is an important precursor to the painful tribal rite of circumcision which initiates boys into adulthood. The description that Laye gives in chapter seven of his novel is like the incident of Big Fadda taking off the head of the *Kibarankoh*.

Tradition and Secrecy

It was part of growing up in a typical village in Nso to be drilled in the culture of traditional secret societies whose membership had nothing occultic but was testimonial of growth into manhood on which depended the security of the tribe. This was tested first and foremost, not just by physical growth and age, but very largely by the ability to keep secrets. A man was not considered a man if he could not keep

secrets. This was as important as the secrets themselves; even open secrets, still had to be kept secret
under the same obligation, for a flippant society is a
lost one.

This background has something positive to offer
when it comes to the evangelization of peoples and
precisely in the formation of candidates for the
priesthood. It is easier to form a culturally mature
young man who has been drilled in the traditional
understanding of secrecy. Forming him to keep con-
fessional secrets and handling matters of the internal
forum thus becomes an issue of reference rather than
initiation. These are areas that inculturation is supposed to exploit for the growth of the faith. Forming
a man without a culture is worse than *The Taming of
the Shrew*. St. Paul equally found it easier to preach
in the city of Athens because it had a culture that he
could use by having recourse to the Greek myth of an
unknown god to teach the Greeks about the known
God:

> For as I walked around and looked carefully
> at your objects of worship, I even found an altar

with this inscription: to an unknown god. So you are ignorant of the very thing you worship—and this is what I am going to proclaim to you. (Acts 17:23)

Accordingly, Sir Winston Churchill said: "A love for tradition has never weakened a nation, indeed it has strengthened nations in their hour of peril." This could be paraphrased to: "A love for tradition has never weakened a *religion*, indeed it has strengthened *religions* in their hour of peril." Pope John Paul II recognized such an inter-relationship between Church and tradition, religion and culture, when he addressed the Aborigines and Torres Strait Islanders in Blatherskite Park during his 1986 pilgrimage in Australia. His address was also a challenge for the Church to safeguard and protect the sacredness of cultures and traditions against secularism. He said:

Your culture, which shows the lasting genius and dignity of your race, must not be allowed to disappear. Do not think that your gifts are worth so little that you should no longer bother to maintain them. Share them with each other and teach them to your children. Your songs, your stories, your paintings, your dances, your languages, must never be lost.[4]

It is rather unfortunate, that the music produced by some of the traditional secret societies we have, like the Nwerong and the Ngiri, is so irresistible and enticing to dance, but people are not free to dance openly in the public. Everyone can only have the listening pleasure, maybe, because there is no way to close the ears of non-members from hearing. The music can be so emotional as to make men cry, such as happened to Fai woo Wan Shilun. He was seen by many people, crying, and sobbing as one would see few men do, all the way from his farm to his compound, talking to himself and holding his head and shaking it in his hands with deep emotions. A little crowd soon gathered behind him, wondering if all

---

[4] John Paul II, "Address to the Aborigines and Torres Strait Islanders in Blatherskite Park" 1986 during his pilgrimage in Australia in 1986.

was well. Had he lost someone in the family? Was he sick? No one dared to ask, but they followed him to get the root cause of what was happening when he reached home. He reached home, went in, washed his face, changed from his farm clothes to his "palace attires," took his palm wine drinking cup and bag, and emerged tear-faced before a crowd that demanded to know what was wrong.

"Wrong?" He asked them, holding his ears in wonder to the question. "Wrong? Do you mean to tell me you are not hearing the voice of Nwerong Nkar?" All was silent, as everyone listened. Indeed, it was the voice of Nwerong Nkar sounding plaintively from the palace. "And you hear Nwerong Nkar speaking in the Nkar language, and yet remain so dry-headed that you don't cry?" He was more surprised at the people for not crying than they were at him for crying. The normal thing is to sing the Nwerong tone, not cry. But that day, Fai woo Wan Shilun was moved but to tears. And he left the bewildered crowd stranded in his courtyard while he headed for the Nwerong place. They felt so foolish and stupid. Somebody suggested that they should hold him and beat him up. But *woo* Wan Shilun was gone.

While in Nkar, Scratch Deeper

Rather than raise a wall, the people of ancient Nkar dug but a long trench round their residential settlement as a means of security. It is believed today that a lot of artifacts from their blacksmithing industry lie buried in some of the centuries-old heaps of black stones that one can still see in Kov Nkar today. Hence the observation that if one is looking for something in Nkar, one must scratch or dig deep for it.

As a young seminarian gathering data for my dissertation on the practice of ululation among the Nkar people that was to serve as partial fulfillment of the requirements for my first degree in Philosophy in 1993, I discovered that element of my people's character and learned never to take anything at face value in Nkar. My visit to one of the elderly and high-ranking notables of the village to get information about the defunct Nkar language proved the point that secrecy had become more of a habit than a discipline for him. He had a copy of M.D.W. Jeffreys' article with scientific information on how the Nkar language died. The article was published in *African Studies* (1945) as "The Death of a Dialect." My informant treated the copy of this article as if it were a *Nwerong* secret. I later learned he thought he was the only one with written material about the Nkar language, which was said, he got from a renowned library in Germany. He was therefore the only man in the village who could be consulted as far as the written remnants of the Nkar language were concerned; as he would later claim, not even the Fon had a copy. Yet this was an article already published in *African Studies* for all to access and read, way back in 1945, but got into the hands of myth. Such is the harm that myth can cause to legend.

When I came back a year later, brandishing a copy of my thesis with information on the Nkar language, which I got from that same article of M.D.W. Jeffreys, that was when my village informant went into the inner chambers of his home and brought out a copy of the article to the light of the sun for everyone standing there to see. Too late! The snare had been broken and the gesture had no impact anymore. He didn't look like a hero in the eyes of bystanders, but like a little boy with a broken toy. Since then, I have tried to publicize that article as much as possible in the struggle against ignorance perpetuated by unproductive myth.

Bongfen Chem-Langhëë had a similar difficulty to get information concerning the transfer of power and authority in Nkar palace. He thinks this might probably owe to the fact that the Nkar fondom got encircled by the Nso people and ended up even losing its language due to that encirclement and socialization. They therefore devised methods of speaking in Lamnso without the rest of the Nso people understanding by using peculiar idioms and sayings.[5] Chem-Langhëë wrote:

---

[5] The present Fon Moloh II of Nkar explained this as the background to the saying: "A yen fo wirnso yuh" (Make sure a Nso person does not hear it), although spoken in Lamnso. It was an Nkar people caution-saying.

I spent the last two weeks of December 1985 and the first week of January 1986 shuttling between Kimbo, Ngkar and Jakiri in a vain attempt to collect oral information for the study. None of the rendezvous I made with potential Ngkar informants was ever honoured. Individual persons I confronted on the spot would not even answer my questions. In the course of these unremitting and unfruitful attempts, one lineage head…who is also an important functionary of the palace…informed me that no individual Ngkar person, acting on his own, would volunteer any information. He advised me to approach the Fon or chief of Ngkar with my problem.[6]

Chem-Langhëë concluded from his frustration that:

---

[6] Bongfen Chem-Langhëë, "The Transfer of Power and Authority in Nto' Ngkar," *Nso' and Its Neighbours: Readings in Social History*, edited by B. Chem-Langhëë and V.G. Fanso, assisted by M. Coheen and E. M. Chilver (from printed manuscripts of 1987), 313.

It seems that either the people of Ngkar are suspicious of researchers or they are unwilling to volunteer information about their customs and themselves. Thus the impatient researcher, particularly one who wants quick results, is warned off Ngkar. However, my experience suggests that, the patient and innocent researcher can always temper their unwillingness to be cooperative.[7]

Although considered as an integrated part of the Nsɔ people today, the Nkar people, nevertheless, have retained most of their unique customs to date, which is best expressed in Pidgin-English as: "Nkar man na Nkar man," meaning, "You can take a man out of Nkar, but you cannot take Nkar out of him."

---

[7] Ibid., 316.

LEGEND ONE

Nkar Church and the Priest
who Harnessed the Devil

"As long as the Nkar Church."

The construction of the Catholic church in Nkar constitutes one of the historical myths in the village. It is one of those myths that developed into legend, as it took an unprecedentedly longer period to build the St. Mary's Parish Church in Nkar, until it became a proverbial saying, "As long as the Nkar Church."

Although it is big in size, the saying nevertheless refers but to the length of time it took to construct the church rather than its physical length. Many stories abound as to what caused the abnormal delay in the construction of this church, but the most interesting account is that of the devil that was captured and placed in a bottle by the parish priest before any progress could be made with the church construction. It sounds like a cousin narrative to *The Bottle Imp*.

Construction work on this legendary church was begun in the late nineteen fifties by the Mill Hill Missionary Priest Fr Wynand Nelissen. He was appointed as the first parish priest (Big Father) of Nkar in 1948 and was nicknamed variously, as Fara Nji and Fara Ngumleejoh by the people, most likely, because of the rough demeanour and the poor treatment he used to give them, kicking them in the back and calling them black monkeys. There was very little difference between him and the colonial masters as far as the relationship and treatment of people was concerned. The people of Nkar remember that part of him more than any of the good works he did for them, including the construction of their parish church. Fr Charles Berinyuy recalls:

> Fr Nelissen spent quite some time in Nkar parish as parish Priest. He built a Fathers' House into which the Fathers moved on Pentecost Sunday, 1951. He built a small church and later on, started a bigger, permanent church in 1956, that proceeded at snail speed. By the time of his departure in 1960, the main section had been completed. It was only in 1966 that the entire Church was completed and inaugurated. Some people suggested that the construction took such a long time because the Priest did not want to be transferred from Nkar.[8]

People say that Fara Nji was so resentful of his transfer from Nkar that he carried away the window-panes and glasses meant for the new church to

---

[8] Charles Berinyuy, The Mill Hill Missionaries in Cameroon: 1922-2022 (Bamenda: Destiny Prints, 2022), 220.

Muyuka where he was transferred. Despite the eventual inauguration in 1966, the church of Nkar was never considered as completed yet, one way or the other, until 2008, when Fr Oliver Shey Ndi carried out some bold renovations that gave it a smarter look. This made Bishop George Nkuo acclaim with a tint of humour that the church of Nkar could now be said to have been completed. What was begun by Fara Nji in 1956 was completed by Fara Ndi in 2008, "as the Lord has assigned to each his task" (1 Cor 3:5).

St. Mary's Church Nkar is one of the principal churches in the Diocese of Kumbo. Events leading to its construction were as mystical as they were physical, humorous, and even manipulative. Kenjo Jumbam narrates the role that Big Father's sunglasses played in getting the people to dig piles and piles of stones, probably for the construction of the first parish church that was much smaller in size than the famous "long" one:

> Big Father was very angry with the people of Mensai because theirs was the smallest. He had invited the catechist of Mensai and Pa Matiu and

scolded them very severely…He paced up and down, occasionally growling like an angry dog. You could see the catechist of Mensai moving uneasily from group to group and answering 'Fadda' each time Big Father growled. It was evident that the people did not understand whatever the Father grunted but were most willing to please him.

After some time he shouted at the people to stop work and listen. Then he went to the shrub that grew nearby and removed his sun-glasses and hung them on it, and put his hat on it. He pointed at it and spoke with force, shaking his forefinger before him a threatening warning. He removed a handkerchief from his pocket and wiped the sweat from his brow and spoke again threateningly, opening wide his eyes from deep down the valley of his face.

The catechist interpreted, 'He says that he wants to go to his house and eat. But before going he has left his eyes to see which people will grow lazy. You can see them on that shrub.'

The people fell to work once more and worked with the same energy as before. But this time they talked, because although Big Father had left his eyes to supervise the work, he had not left his ears. So anybody talking turned his back on the eyes. They worked until their backs ached and their hands got blisters, and they urged the catechist to go and tell Big Father that they were tired. He went timidly and saw the houseboy who told him that Big Father was taking his siesta. And the people of Mensai continued to work and they worked without a break until the sun had gone down in the west and shadows were becoming long.

Then Big Father came and took his eyes and his hat and he waved at them to go away.[9]

At that time, St. Mary's Parish Nkar covered as far as Djottin, Elak, Mbessa, Mbam, Ebal, Buu, Jakiri, Wainama, Vekovi, and Sop which are present-day

---

[9] Kenjo Jumbam, *The White Man of God* (London: Heinemann Educational Books Inc., 1980), 92-93.

parishes or pastoral zones with resident priests. Christians came from all over these places to carry stones, sand, wood, and cement on their heads for the construction of the main parish church. There are claims that there was a tractor available to carry these things, faster and better, but making the Christians carry them on the head seemed to match with Fara Nji's manipulations to prolong the construction of the church. It could take a good five miles to and from Taatiy (the stone mountain) from where all the stones used in that construction were quarried and carried to the building site, but Fara Nji would rather have the people carry them on the head. It is said that he also had eight men carry a heavily assembled scarfold for the building of the church all the way from the cattle ranch after Jakiri, some seven miles away. They were strong Christians though—so strong, some of them could do three trips of stone carrying in a day, and still walk ten or more miles back to their home stations. Those were feats of physical power performed for the spiritual salvation of their souls. Other feats were reportedly more mystical, involving the devil and his gang of demons.

When people get weary of conditions and circumstances, they can also become vulnerable and susceptible to fears and suspicions. The devil takes advantage of such moments to weaken their faith in God. The Jews knew better about such experiences in their journey from Egypt to the Promised Land when they turned even to a molten calf for protection and provision. That is what happened to the people of Nkar when the construction of the church took so long to be realized. A story soon circulated that the devil was attacking the church construction and that there was a particular area in which he had made his habitat on the building so that, each time it was constructed, it collapsed. The demon assigned by Satan to attack the church project was also said to be relocating the stones that were carried by the Christians back to the quarry, and it was only after capturing and placing the demon in a bottle that the stones could be successfully transported to the construction site.

The story followed a logical pattern, that no sooner did the Christians reach their homes following a tedious transportation of stones, than they got news from Nkar that nothing was left of the heaps of stones they had piled a day or two before. After repeated reports of the fast "disappearance" of stones from the building site, word soon started to circulate among people in distant missions that someone was relocating the stones from the building site to the quarry. There were even claims that some stones were marked at the building site one evening and they disappeared overnight, only to be found the following day in the quarry at Taatiy. This was clearly the work of an invisible hand, the work of the devil, for Pa Watchnight could not notice anything, although as an experienced night watch he recalled that there were some nights, while at work, when he had dreams about something weird happening around the church building. But he never saw anything nor anyone. Therefore, it must be the devil. And now the one-million-dollar question was: Who was going to harness this devil?

Fara Nji was champion of physical brutality and mistreatment of the people. Could he be match for the devil at all? Could he also kick the bottom of Satan and curse him out of the church project in the

Dutch language in the same way as he did to the people? This was a task that required more of spiritual and mystical fitness than kicking people's bottoms.

The priest, however, is said to have gone on leave to his native country and come back fortified and ready to face the devil. On the day of the contest, everyone prayed and fasted and then went over to Taatiy where this powerful Dutch priest surveyed the devil's physical manifestation and discovered that it was in the form of a black ant. He then transformed into a black ant also, placed a special bottle he had brought from the Whiteman's country, and challenged the demonic ant to a contest. He first got into the bottle and came out, and the demon also got in and came out. Then he got in and came out again, and the demon did the same. This went on from morning till evening, as the Christians prayed harder and harder. It was a tough contest, at the end of which, the priest succeeded to exhaust the demon, and when he went in and out again one more time, and the demon went in, he corked it in the bottle, and brought it back to the church. Christians from everywhere gathered and watched at the demon going round and round in the bottle in the form of an ant, unable to come out. Thus did this powerful priest, like St. Michael the Archangel, overpower the devil at Taatiiy, before St. Mary's Parish Church Nkar could be built. But when you ask:

"What became of the bottle and the demonic ant?" No answer.

"Who actually saw this demonic ant in the bottle?" No answer.

"Who actually participated in the prayer and fasting session at Taatiy?" No answer.

But the story resolves the riddle of the "long church" in Nkar. That is the nature of myth, and that is the purpose that myth is meant to serve. It provokes questions whose answers are not welcome. Where mathematics stops, myth gladly takes over. This Nkar myth could not calculate scientifically, that the number of stones carried within a certain amount of time by a group of people would require far less time for one mason to exhaust the heap of stones that might have taken the group hours to transport from the quarry to the building site. One could spend an entire day of eight hours to carry four big stones that would take the builder an average of ten minutes to use all of them. That arithmetic was offensive to the people's energy, and the conclusion was very traditional of myth–someone must be accused of liquidating the stones, somehow, and it couldn't be anyone else than the devil himself, "the accuser of the brethren" (Rev 12:10). But from the background stories of why it took so long to construct the church in Nkar, Professor Francis Mbuntum acutely summarized from a mathematical perspective that there were certainly more than just one devil to harness and that the list could be "As long as the Nkar Church."

LEGEND TWO

The Menang Dance and the Visit to Paris

Among the earliest people to go abroad to Europe from Nkar village were the famous Menang dancers, most of whom were unlettered men who could barely write their names. The Menang dance, known in Nkar as Menang *mee* Rohmbii, was founded by a man called Menang whose job was to watch over ripe crops from attacks by pests. He was the eldest son of the Rohmbii family and seemed to have gotten his inspiration from watching at the millet and corn swaying in dance to the winds, as the costume of the dancers matched with the tone of the farm nature in many respects and aspects. This dance grew and won fame in the 1950s through to the 70s, as the most dexterous and entertaining traditional dance in Cameroon. It was invited to Lagos to receive Queen Elizabeth II in 1956 during Her Majesty's 20-day imperial visit to Nigeria. Seven years later, if there was a way for France to assimilate the Menang dancers as they have done to African footballers, most of the dancers would have become French citizens in 1963 when the French President General Charles de Gaulle invited the raffia-skirt-and-blouse dancers from *Graffiland* to thrill and mesmerise the people of Paris with their dancing skills and music.

In those days in Cameroon, merit still had the authority of right; otherwise, if it were today, those dancers would not have moved an inch out of the village of Nkar. Their deserving spirit took them to Dakar in Senegal to entertain representatives from 18 French-speaking African nations at the fourth French African summit. While in France, their performance was extended to Bonn in Germany. And one cannot count the number of times this dance from Nkar in Southern Cameroon went to Yaounde to entertain international guests. But like other resources of English-speaking Cameroon, the dance and the dancers were used, exhausted, and dumped like the stump of the legendary broom, lying ingloriously in one corner of the house after it has been used to keep every other thing clean except itself. All that the dancers had to show were tape recorders, some of which had to be wound manually, and some old suits, which many sold away for a beer, or to settle hospital bills in the days of misery. No photos to show, no money to live on, but they have the fame and honour of where they went and whom they saw, even if they exaggerate, for we do not forget that they came from Nkar.

The government of Cameroon owes Nkar village the acknowledgement, revival, and honour of the Menang dance and dancers. In the same manner, the people of Rohmbii compound who owned this dance owe the Nkar people and deserve some lashes of the whip for letting the dance die at the village level. Similar sanctions need to be meted on the Taadui family in Nkar for also letting the Njuh dance die a similar death. The sound of the drum from this dance and its whistle used to descend on the village in a good moonlit night like a spell. Its drumming could be heard resounding through Kov Nkar, way beyond midnight, keeping everyone happily awake, as Mah-Njuh sent her voice piercing through the night with lyrics:

Heli heli helicopter!
My brother is coming with helicopter!
I have no time to speak with you!
I have no time to talk to you!
Heli heli helicopter!

When it was time for the Shuufai of Taadui to come out to dance, the ambiance was such that if you weren't from Taadui family, you would, at least, want to be friends with someone from there. Shuufai Taadui was a man endowed with a dignity so original and natural that when you met with him on the way, you could sense the royal spirit beaming tangibly from his personality. The families of Taadui and Rohmbii owe the people of Nkar the revival of these legendary legacies–the Njuh and the Menang dances respectively.

The setup of the Menang dance included every-thing beautiful and required all the energy a young man could offer. The music from the xylophone, the drum, the gong, the rattles, etc., produced such a eu-phoric harmony that made old people forget their ages and the sick swerve in their sickbeds. The dancers comprised a maiden juju called *Wanle Ngon Shinang* that danced beside the xylophone with a horse-tail whisk. There was also a rascally juju called *Nton* that did not follow any pattern of dancing style but played calculated and entertaining mischief and villainy on others, especially on the maiden dancer, by trying to touch *her* breasts. It was a systematic distractor whose attire of a black gown matched its role. The major dancers wore short skirts and blouses made from raffia leaves and a flamboyant head that was an imitation of the forest lily that grows typically in Kov Nkar known as *Kiyayuhyah*. The captain, known as *Kam*, who carried a staff in hand and had a more elegant costume of a big gown also made from raffia leaves, set the tone of the entire dance in a similar manner as the main celebrant does at the celebration of Holy Mass. The success of the dance depended very much on the performance of the *Kam*.

The Menang dance became an intimate part of Nkar culture. It was almost part of the primary school curriculum, and no traditional dance could beat the Menang dance from St. Mary's School Nkar when it came to school dance competitions. Traditionally, it is a men's dance, but in school, both girls and boys participated with Yaana woo Ntongki playing the xylophone for the boys to dance. Excelling in Menang, rather than in academics, fetched a full sponsorship in Pa Yong's Comprehensive High School (CHS) Bambui for the renowned school *Kam Menang*, Francis Fai Nchadzee, alongside three fellow dancers who were given partial sponsorship. The proprietor of CHS Bambui, Pa Yong, came himself to offer the package of fame to the young dancers whose names had reached far and beyond the village again! He wanted to have the dance in his school and was ready to do for the school children what the government didn't do for their fathers.

At the height of its popularity, the Menang dance from Nkar had two major rivals, namely the Menang of Maamo from Kumbo and *Shitiy* from Kinsenjam. The Menang of Maamo had more political powers as the dance from the central town of Kumbo, but merit and not politics was what was needed for entertainment. While the Shitiy from Kinsenjam led by Ibrai Nkem posed as an authentic challenger on the dancing ground, the *Kam Menang* from Nkar proved himself even more legendry and indomitable with creative skills. Elias Kwahndzeh could run a mile with the rattles on his ankles and no one would hear them make a single sound. He was so much in control of them that the rattles seemed to understand and obey him when he merely looked at them. He led the Menang of Rohmbii to places no one from Nkar had been before. He was not only a gifted dancer but also commanded a prompt sense of time management very unlike Africa, which thrilled and enchanted Europeans who believed that Africans do things in time and not on time. If the Menang was given fifteen minutes to perform, Elias Kwahndzeh could coordinate the entire performance and pull it to a stop by a few seconds to the minute. And he could do all of that without a watch. He and his mates also incorporated some of the best dancing styles of the Shitiy, which made the Shitiy redundant. Many times, after a competition, the Menang dance was often requested to dance again, just for entertainment, after the rest of the dances had retired.

Excelling in traditional music and dancing was a gift that was generally endowed on the Nkar people.

If you hailed from Nkar, then you had to be good in one traditional dance or the other. And if you couldn't dance like Boni and Kuhnsah, then you could sing for others to dance like George Wirba and Chin Congo. It gradually became common, wherever there were children from Nkar, to have traditional dances for cultural entertainment, even in female religious communities. Fr. Aloysius Balon Wankui, the first native priest of the British Cameroons, is remembered as a quintessence of a *Njang* dancer. Archbishop Paul Verdzekov recalls: "Those who knew Father Wankuy will probably remember that he knew very well, thoroughly enjoyed, and could dance with admirable grace and elegance, the Kom traditional dance, Njang."[10] And he hailed from Nkar.

As the saint teaches, grace builds on nature. Therefore, genius always comes from the perspiration of inspiration. Accordingly, the Menang dance

---

[10] Paul Verdzekov, "Sixtieth Anniversary of the Priestly Ordination of Father Aloysius Balon Wankuy," (unpublished, 1 July 2009), Ntasin-Bamenda.

had regular practice, at least five times a week, under the shed of the great *Mbii* tree from which the Rohm-bii compound that had this dance took its family name. The tree also became legendary as the largest and oldest tree in the village. Its shed spread to almost a square kilometre, producing millions of black edible berries called *mbii*. This fruit-bearing tree is said to have been brought and planted in Nkar by one of the princes called Mbii who was a trader and brought the fruit with some of its seeds from one of his journeys to neighbouring Bamoum land. The fruit was named after him, and when he ascended the throne as the Fon of Nkar, this great tree became the royal tree from which princes and princesses ate. When it fell due to age, it was accorded traditional mourning rights like that of a high-ranking noble in Nkar, commemorated for eight days, during which no one went to the farm and there were juju displays. This was the Fon's tree, and it was from under this tree that Nkar became famous by the Menang dance.

Africans seem to be at their best with technology when it comes to designing jujus and masquerades. Even children tend to manifest creative abilities through the little jujus they conceive and make. Nigeria has some of the most expensive jujus in the world, designed by minds of great architectural creativity. Sometimes, the juju technology makes one wonder if the designer was any less inspired than was Michelangelo in designing the Pieta. There are jujus designed to display from engineering principles and operations. Unfortunately, the juju-technology tends to be referred to as witchcraft, not science, and is made to look mystical and metaphysical, even when it is pure physics.

While in Paris, the gentlemen from Nkar were each given two pairs of suits and two pairs of black shoes. They looked cute and international. Each person was also given some French francs, in notes and coins. The notes were for pocket money and the coins for public toilets. Pocket money was understandable, but to pay for the use of a toilet was almost the same as paying for sh*t when back home one could even go behind the house and use the latrine before coming to greet the houseowner. What would the Fon of Nkar and Nwerong say when they hear such a thing? More so, a single visit to the toilet could cost enough to buy a litter of palm oil back home. And to make matters worse, there was no bush or forest within easy reach. Everyone was wondering and figuring out possibilities of how to save the sh*t money. That was when Tamfu Viban came up with a bright idea similar in structure to the one that Caiaphas gave the Jews about Jesus, that it was better for one man to die than for a whole nation to perish. Everyone subscribed to it, that it was better to use one coin for everyone to visit the toilet than to throw away money.

Accordingly, it was agreed that everyone would go to the toilet at the same time twice a day, in the morning and in the evening. In that way, they would use only one coin for the service of everyone. If you are looking for practical mathematicians, Nkar is the place. The smart plan was to wedge the toilet door with a rock once the first person had gone in, and then the rest would follow one after another. Unfortunately, they looked everywhere and could not find a little rock to use. Then someone suggested that a shoe could do the trick. Just one shoe was enough. Since it was Tamfu's idea, and he was a man who never looked away from a challenge, the lots fell on him by free option. Tamfu went in first, did his business, removed one of his black French shoes, and wedged the door with it. The results were disastrous, for as soon as he stepped out, the electric door slammed back automatically, mercilessly trimming Tamfu's shoe into two pitiful halves. The Menang dance brought so much fame and novelty to Nkar village.

Menang Dances

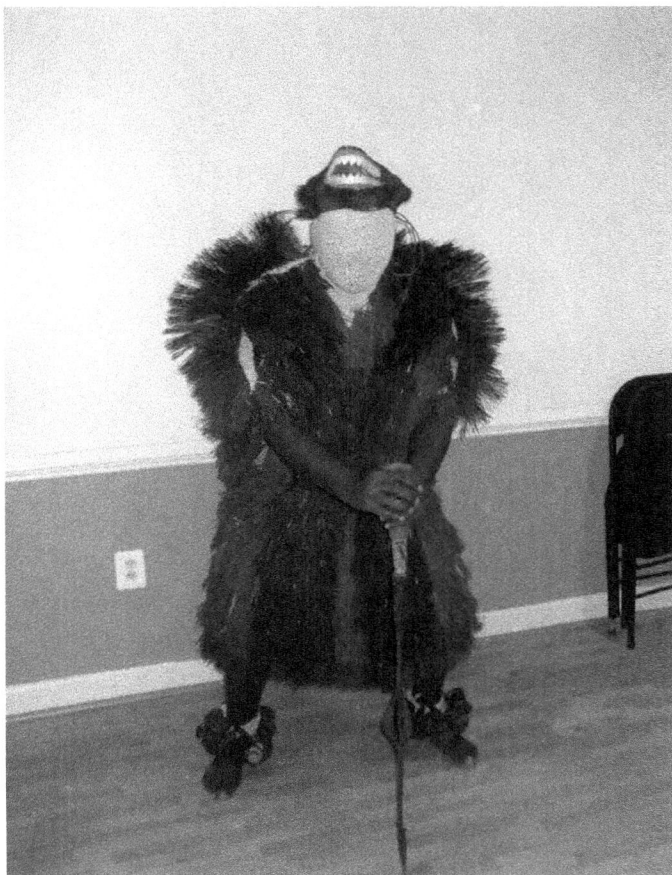

Kam Menang (Captain)

LEGEND THREE

Tamfu brought the Sea to Nkar

In Chinua Achebe's celebrated novel *Things Fall Apart*, the author recounts: "As the *egwugwu* approach the stools, Okonkwo's wives notice that the second *egwugwu* walks with the springy step of Okonkwo and also that Okonkwo is not seated among the elders, but of course, they say nothing about this odd coincidence." Such odd coincidences were common with Tamfu and many jujus in Nkar, so many indeed, that one would be daring too much to say something about the coincidences. But in his days, many jujus exhibited a stout agility in their manner of display that had semblance to Tamfu's structure and statue, his physical strength, and daredevil ventures.

Tamfu did not only travel abroad, but he also helped his village folks to see the sea by carrying some of its waters in a little bottle, which he brought home for everyone to see. Since everyone could not go to see the sea, Tamfu brought the sea to come see them. The news circulated so fast around the village, when the dancers returned from Europe, that Tamfu, also known as Baa Yuka, had brought the sea with him from abroad. There was no emphasis that it was sea water in a bottle; the news was rather that he had brought the sea itself. And people came from far and near to see the sea in Tamfu's house. The curiosity to see the sea got many children into trouble with their parents, as they got enticed in the temptation of fetching firewood on Sunday, or picking kola nuts in the forest, or carrying water for Tamfu's household, when they had done nothing of the like in their own homes, just to please Tamfu to bring out the sea for them to see.

Village social entertainment and animation consisted basically in football matches and watching jujus, which did not happen often unless someone connected to them died before they could display. Sometimes children did not care to hide their wishes for someone connected to the jujus to die so that they would display. If it was a high-ranking traditional ruler or a prince or princess, that was the best, for that would mean a weeklong display of all the jujus in the palace. Tamfu's sea was therefore a great event, comparable to a juju display. Sunday was the day he always brought the sea out from the cupboard around evening time when the church bell for Benediction would be chiming and whining through the quiet groves of Kov Nkar. If by then Tamfu was pleased with the heaps of wood, or kola nuts, or the buckets of water presented as fee for the sea-show, he would come out and look at the position of the sun in the sky, as if to determine whether the tides were low or high enough for the sea to come out. And the stories would begin. True or false, who cared. Besides, who knew better to challenge Tamfu, when the largest body of water anyone had ever seen was the Tsemkan whose waters could sometimes dry up completely in a harsh dry season.

Tamfu explained that the sea was like a person, only of a different kind. It had its own home with creatures living in it like a family. It went on journeys, ate, and drank from fresh streams and rivers. Wow! It could get happy and calm, but when angry, it could become very nasty and rough, hitting its head on the banks and shores, fuming with rage, and swallowing anything within its reach. That was frightful. You could not listen to all that stuff from Tamfu without forgetting to close your mouth. He would then go on to describe the big fish that lived in the sea as if it was just one of its kind. This fish, he said, was bigger than the one that swallowed Jonah in the Bible. It was as big as the Nkar Church. And if something was bigger than the Nkar Church, then it could not be measured. Occasionally, this fish would choose a village or town of its liking and honour it with its meat by exposing its belly for people to cut as much meat as they wanted for their families. It could be there for weeks. The bad side of this generosity by this fish was that, on the day of its departure, it would take some people along to go and eat and fill up the lost meat. That didn't sound so good of that big fish. If it gave meat, say, to Victoria, people would come from as far as Ngaoundere, Garoua, Maroua, even Kousseri in the North of Cameroon to cut it. Another very interesting character of the sea was that those who live close to it never bother about buying salt.

They just get water from the sea because it is salt water.

In the later years, when I first saw the Atlantic Ocean, the big brother of the sea, I realized immediately, that there was no way any of us could ever have seen the sea as it is from the bottle. However, Tamfu's theory helped me to better understand the doctrine of the Incarnation by providing me with an analogy, that God also became man by compacting himself in the confines of Jesus of Nazareth, yet one substance with the Father in the same manner as Tamfu's sea water in the bottle remained one in substance with the big water from which it came: a microcosm of a macrocosm. Those who saw Jesus of Nazareth in person really experienced him as "God from God, Light from Light, true God from true God, begotten not made, one in being with the Father." Yet, those who saw him still had to go to heaven to see God as he really is, in the same manner as those who saw the sea in the bottle still had to go and see it in its immensity. No doubt, those who came from the coast and who had seen the ocean were respected in almost the same way as those who had been abroad to Europe and

America. When Lemali of Kinkahdzeh returned from visiting his little sister who lived down the coast in Victoria, he was received by a traditional dance that entertained those who had gathered to receive him for the whole night in his honour, while he sat in one corner of the house wearing a neat white shirt and a coloured scarf around his neck, drinking "33" Stout, the beer of the time, because he had been to the coast, and had seen the sea.

LEGEND FOUR

The Football Match between Men and Women

All sorts of strange stories used to come from the coast. Among them was that of the defence football player in Victoria who kicked the ball so high into the sky during a football match among plantation workers that they waited for minutes only to see but the ashes coming down from the sky. The sun had burnt it!

The football match that took place in Nkar in the early 1970s between the men and women had events that were as fabulous in size as those of the match in Victoria. At that match, Shey Visovkui distinguished himself as the village goalkeeper for the men while Tavkinang narrowly missed being the man of the match. The match lasted for one hour, at the end of which, almost every player on the men's side had been replaced, except for Shey Visovkui the goalkeeper and Tavkinang the defence man also known as home-back.

While the women were jogging and exercising prior to the match, the men sat at one corner of the field and emptied a jug of palm wine in preparation for the match. The results were obvious: 1-0 in favour of the women. The goal came in from a penalty kick caused by Tavkinang. The match was getting to an end on a goalless draw, when a young, determined attacker from the women's side came with the ball and dribbled through the defence players. Tavkinang was the last hope, but she dribbled and passed him with ease. As the home-back, Tavkinang had to do something. He ran after her and dived for the ball right in the goal-area. That cost Tavkinang two heavy prizes – a penalty that led to the men's defeat and the nomination as the man of the match, as he was the favourite player of the day.

When the ball was placed on the penalty spot, goalkeeper Shey Visovkui left the goalpost and came and stood right in front of the ball to block the kick. The referee took him back with some difficulties and instructed him that he was not to move until the whistle had been blown. Shey was wearing a big agbada gown, which he opened **wide by stretching** his arms. The whistle went, and the kick was taken. The ball rolled gently and passed over the goal line not too far away from Goalkeeper Shey, as everyone shouted: "Koooh Shey! Koooh Shey!" (Catch it, Shey! Catch it, Shey!) Shey stayed put, and only stretched his right hand toward the ball and never shook from where the referee had stationed him and told him not to move. And that was how the women defeated the men. If that match had gone beyond one hour, someone would have collapsed.

LEGEND FIVE

The Mental Lady that Stopped the Liturgy

Besides the length of time that it took to construct St. Mary's Church Nkar, this church is also noted for dramatic events. It was in Nkar church that the inculturation of liturgical music started in Nso land when Chia Paul Ntumpku introduced the xylophone with drums and some other traditional components and rhythms. His famous Lamnso Mass commonly known as *Tata sham mendzen* (Lord have mercy), drew both Christians and non-Christians from far and near to attend the early Sunday Mass in Nkar, just to listen to Chia Paul intone *Tata sham mendzoen* with the xylophone.

Everything went on well until a mentally overcharged lady also heard from far away what was happening in Nkar and came to see for herself. As the xylophone sounded the notes gently to the delight of everyone, the guest-lady got up from her seat and listened unbelievably before taking the assembly hostage with: "Stop! Stop it! I say, stop it!" And indeed, everything stopped, as she tied the wrapper firmer around her waist and moved forward threateningly towards the priest on the altar, stopping just one step short of ascending, and addressed the stunned Fr. Figl who was considered the legend of the faith in Nkar and beyond:

Fada! Whetti I am hear for church? Njangi de dance for church? I de ask na you: Njangi de dance for church? The last day eeeh! Make I no hear'em again. Take'm go dance for schoolyard. You hear?" (Father, what is this that I am hearing in the church? Club music in the church? It's you I am asking: Club music in the church? This should be the last day! Let me not hear it again. Take it out to the schoolyard. Have you heard?)

It was this same great choir music that caused someone's trousers to give way in church during offertory, as he danced to the altar with a bunch of plantains on his shoulders. The rope holding his trousers just gave way, and they came tumbling down in a jumble at the middle of the aisle. He was caught between catching the trousers and the bunch of plantains from falling, and he chose to save God's bunch of plantains, letting the trousers drop. After all, on the Last Day, God will judge him from his gift and not from his dressing.

It was not long after this incident, that a similar one happened, when a delicately padded behind of one of the elegantly dressed ladies gave way and dropped off to the floor as she danced her way to present her gift at the altar. One of her handmade buttocks just fell off. She took a leave of absence from the village for almost a year, until the village healed from the incident. It proved the Scriptures true that: "If the Lord does not build the house, in vain does the builder labour" (Ps 127:1).

LEGEND SIX

Joseph Taanya and Fr. Michael de Rooy

My uncle, Joe Taanya was one of the selected men to travel abroad for the Menang dance, but he missed the bus to Yaounde by a few minutes and chased after it on foot. The following day, when a plane happened to fly over the village, he gave chase after it again, calling for it to stop and take him. Missing such an opportunity could drive someone nuts.

How he got the name Taanya, or simply Nya, for short, he himself could not recall, but in his days of youthful exuberance, Joe Nya was a household name in Kov Nkar, so much that he once complained, even toads and frogs were calling his name everywhere he passed: "Nya! Nya! everywhere," he said.

Joe Nya was a troublesome young man. He was the type of man who always found reason for swimming upstream even if there was gold downstream. He was a man attracted by extraordinary things, even danger. The famous Fara Nji was his archenemy. Fr.

Michael de Rooy did not find Joe a "yes-Father-man" either and referred to him as *kata-kata* man (Problem man). That was deserving, for Fr. De Rooy had gone out of his way to bring the statue of the Blessed Mother all the way from his home country in The Netherlands. Christians flocked to the church to see the new statue of the patroness of their church before it was raised to stand at its permanent position. The instructions for the visits were strict and clear: No one should touch the statue. Well, Joe Taanya touched it!

Some children who were present in the church with him ran off immediately and reported the matter to Fr. De Rooy, that Mr. Taanya had touched Maria. Fr. De Rooy did not wait to get the details right, that it was the statue of Mary that Joe had touched against instructions. Knowing Joe for who he was, he immediately concluded that Joe had touched but the breasts of one of the young girls in church. Fr. De Rooy jerked his big trousers to almost chest level, as he fumed down the stairs from his office toward Joe, cursing in his Dutch language, something like: "Pot forr dama! Dama! Joseph Tamnyam! You touchie

Maria he boobi? You kata-kata man! Why you touchie Maria he boobi?"

Joe protested, "Me no touch'em Fada!"

"You been touch'em, Joseph! You been touch'-em! You be some kata-kata man."

The story spread in the village like wildfire, that Joe touched Maria's breasts in church. And many children cried from that because anyone who wanted to cry simply had to call out when Joe was passing anywhere: "You been touch'em!"

The knocks from Joe's flexed fingers could burst one's skull. He was a physically strong man and known to the rest of us in the family as Baa woo Fumbor. This was a respectful address he got from us after his stay in the French-speaking neighbouring town of Foumbot, where he lived for some time cultivating tomatoes and came back with a portable xylophone, which he used to hang around his neck and play while attending to his garden of tomatoes. He also brought some French that he taught us. The one we never forgot was how to greet people in French on New Year's Day. In Foumbot they say: "Bonne annee meveh." It was so many years after, that my elder brother discovered that "meveh" was "mauvaise" meaning "bad" or "terrible" in the sense of hectic. It was probably a reference to how the New Year had been celebrated. Joe did his best to get what he could of that French to us. When he missed the trip to Paris, that whole month was "meveh" for everyone in the village, as he shouted and knocked on any head that was available around him for very little offenses.

When a wildfire from the churchyard came and burnt down his first thatched hut, Joe came to live with us at home. To keep him out of trouble, my dad bought a record player whose name we learned from Baa woo Fumbor as *Gramaphone* (Gramophone). It was operated with a manual disc spinner to produce great music. That was the work of the operator, selecting the plates and generating the energy that played the music. Everything depended on the operator, and whenever the *Gramaphone* was hired for a wedding party, Joe was treated like a prince – Prince Gramaphone.

Eventually, the *Bottle Dance* known as *Kibanteh* came into fashion and was performed live. It knocked the *Gramaphone* out of business, and Joe out of popularity. In response, Joe decided to become notoriously problematic on every occasion of the *Bottle Dance*, which was a pattern dance with rules. Any dancer who missed the steps or did not follow the orders of the conductor was sent out from the dancing floor. One of the rules was "No short nicker." That was a personal affront on Joe whose formal wear comprised a pair of shorts. And Joe would start a fight. He could confront anything, and once stopped someone from receiving Holy Communion in church because the person had something to reconcile with him. He held him back physically: "Sit down. Where are you going to? Have you seen me going there? Or you think I don't have legs with which to walk or a mouth to receive Holy Communion. Sit down. When we fix our issues, all of us can come and receive Taata!" It was *fait accompli*.

When Joe died, the village and the Church in Nkar missed him. It was just right and fitting that his first daughter, Carine Shela, whom he loved so much should become a nun. Joe needed to pay the Church with something dear to him for all the headaches he caused Fara Nji and Fr. Michael de Rooy, and other parish priests in Nkar.

LEGEND SEVEN

Chia John Shang

Thanks to primary school studies of geography and history, many of us came to know and understand that Egypt, Rome, Jerusalem, Galilee, and Nazareth were places on earth. In the catechism classes, Bethlehem sounded as if Jesus was born in heaven and not on earth. Chia John Shang, the catechist, told us stories about these places that made one think they were extraterrestrial. He taught the catechism in such a manner that even if you forgot the lessons of the stories, you never forgot the stories of the lessons. His mouth was always in a chewing mode, and we used to say he was chewing stories, for he never lacked them. We went to doctrine classes, not only for the greatest desire and excitement of receiving Holy Communion, but also to listen to Chia John Shang's stories, some of which were said to come from his participation in the Second World War.

His counterpart was a man in Mbiame, who was also an ex-soldier from the Second World War and told stories that were larger than life itself. It was not easy to ascertain whether he went to Burma, in India, to fight as a soldier during the Second World War or to Jerusalem to pray, as a pilgrim, or both. He highlighted each episode depending on his audience. His visit to Jerusalem took the upper hand when he was with priests. It made him look holier than the rest of mankind in the eyes of the men of God. And when he was with his ordinary village folks, Burma was emphasized, making him look braver than any of them. He claimed, that when he went to Jerusalem and visited Calvary, he walked the exact Way of the Cross as did Jesus: "The Way of the Cross, and not the Stations of the Cross that you people pray here in Mbiame. I walked on the same path that Jesus himself walked, right to Calvary," he would brag. When he arrived at Calvary Hill and was shown the footprint of Jesus, which has remained there to date, he placed his right foot on it, and it fitted exactly to that of Jesus. His right foot was physically the same as that of

Jesus. African Night Entertainment: Mbiame versus Nkar.

When the doctrine bell would chime at four o'clock each evening, children of five years and above, would start finding their way to the cate- chism/story room of Chia John Shang where every- one had a nickname. That was another characteristic of Nkar village. You could not grow up in Nkar with- out a nickname. My grandmother used to warn our cousins from our mother's side in Mbah to be careful when visiting in Nkar, or they will come back with a nickname. We even got confused between our real names and the nick ones. When I went to enrol for the catechism classes, I gave but my corn-fufu name Taandi. The catechist was sure that was not my real name, so he asked if there was any elderly person in the room who knew me. My elder brother Edwin came forward immediately. And when the catechist asked him for his own name, he said his name was Shey, which was also a nickname. In the end, our fa- ther had to write the names on a piece of paper for us to bring with us the following day. But that did not save us from being known all through our childhood days as Shey and Taandi.

The catechism classroom was indeed a gathering of those seeking for salvation. Those with torn dresses held together by strings or ropes from falling apart; those with running noses and tear-stained faces chased from home to the doctrine classes; those with half-eaten cobs of fresh corn, perhaps given as bribe by mothers; catechumens with tails that needed to be trimmed; all found their way into this legendary room, searching for salvation. The confused smell that used to rise from the doctrine classroom needed salvation itself. And every so often, someone would add to the already bad situation. Not a few times were doctrine sessions suspended for everyone to go out and take a breath of fresh air because someone had released unwanted air. Then the witch hunting would begin among bench mates: "It was you. No, it wasn't me." Well, it was someone.

Chia John Shang made us love the Benediction. He taught us the beautiful Latin hymns and other hymns in the dialect, mostly composed by his predecessor Chia Paul Ntumpku. Attending Vespers on

Sundays was a Catholic treat because of the hymns
and the smell of incense. We used to also eat the can-
dle stumps, and, occasionally, Chia John Shang did
give us some old non-consecrated hosts to taste. Very
tasteless. The very aroma from burnt incense felt like
heaven itself as Chia John intoned the *Tantum ergo
Sacramentum.*

Tamfu was not the only person reputed to be in
possession of a strange item, like sea water. It was also
rumoured that Chia John Shang had been to Nine-
veh, the city from which the prophet Jonah was es-
caping from God when the famous big fish was
caused to swallow and keep him in its belly for three
days. That sounded like having been to heaven and
back to earth. He did not help much to clarify any of
the rumours but made matters worse by naming one
of his grandsons Jonas and having the largest fish-
pond in the village. He used to ask the doctrine children to help bring fish feed from their homes–rotten
corn, yams, cassava, house refuse, etc. No one dared
fail to bring some feed for his fish, if not for love of
him as the catechist, then, although never spoken
aloud, for fear of what connections he might have

with the large fish that swallowed Jonah. Chia John Shang was the most punctual man in the village. When he pulled the rope to sound the toll of the church bell, you could correct your watch to half passed five in the morning or four in the evening.

LEGEND EIGHT

William Samka
and the Remote-Controlled Stones

Samka had a nickname that he hated with all his heart. Although he has been long dead and gone for decades now, I still feel the caution of even writing down the name Samka Mendondo. It had the implied meaning of a debtor, which he wasn't. But Samka hated the name with a venom, that if he was playing at the football world cup finals and was about to score the winning goal for Cameroon, and someone called that name, he would prefer to abandon the ball and go but after that person with stones. Children used to stand at a very safe distance before calling or singing it, followed by stones that behaved as if they were remote-controlled. If he shot a stone after you, it never stopped until it hit you. They referred to them as chasing stones because they literally chased you down, and if you took a bend, they would take the same bend until they hit you. There was nothing like "To Whom It May Concern" with William Samka's stones; they went only for those to whom they were concerned and could even dodge those with whom they were not concerned. A stone in his left hand was as dangerous as a pebble in King David's sling. The best thing was always to avoid provoking Samka.

No one could rival Samka in producing bamboo cars with wooden wheels that were pulled manually from a rope and dragged to destinations around the village. He could transport anything portable by his car, such as passengers, wood, mud blocks for the construction of houses, and many other items. Samka loved football with an indomitable passion. He was always the first to arrive at the football field for the daily weekday practice sessions and would be the last to leave. He made his own balls out of banana leaves. And his balls were notoriously heavy. It was rumoured that he used to place a sizeable rock at the middle when composing the banana leaves with ropes acquired from banana suckers. Little children avoided kicking Samka's balls for obvious reasons; it could cost your ankle. Samka was lame in the right hand and right leg, but when he kicked the ball with the left leg, the shots seemed to be fired with compensated energy. Sometimes, as goalkeeper, you would prefer to let Samka's shot pass into the pool than attempt to stop it, especially if the ball was from his industry. When we attended the catechism lessons together, Chia John Shang made Samka the Discipline Prefect (Chief Whip). A function never fitted a man more than the Chief Whip thing fitted Samka. Not a fly could buzz carelessly during lessons. Unfortunately, he paid more attention to this duty than to his doctrine lessons, and at the end of the year, after being examined by Fr. Michael de Rooy, the Chief Whip failed the final exams.

LEGEND NINE

Mammy woo Teri
and Twenty Million Signs of the Cross

Jesus emphasized quality rather than quantity in the things of God, especially prayer. Hence the widow's mite assumed an eternal propensity in God's eyes from its value rather than its quantity. He impressed this teaching on his followers, that what matters before God is the quality of quantity rather than the quantity of quality since with God, "a day is like a thousand years, and a thousand years are like a day" (2 Pt 3:8).

Accordingly, Jesus taught his followers:

> When you pray, do not keep on babbling like pagans, for they think they will be heard because of their many words. Do not be like them, for your Father knows what you need before you ask him. (Mt 6:7-8)

Clara Woolani, popularly known as Mammy woo Teri (Little mother), couldn't care less about the quality of the sign of the cross she made as her form of prayers. She was perhaps the greatest exponent of devotion to making the *Sign of the Cross*. Her only rival in volumes of prayer was Yaa Shamendzen (Grandmother of Mercy) who was another prayer warrior in the village. While Mammy woo Teri championed the Sign of the Cross, Yaa Shamendzen championed the *Stations of the Cross*, which she prayed until they became a hobby rather than a devotion. She used to spend hours of prayer in the church and would go to the farm almost by midday, and after tilling a few ridges, the appetite for prayer would hit her hard again, and she would fashion crosses from sticks and pin them on fourteen ridges in the farm and start with the Stations of the Cross again.

On the other hand, Mammy woo Teri could make an average of ten signs of the cross in a minute, and could go sometimes for thirty minutes nonstop, covering at least 300 signs of the cross. Her intermediary break sessions during Mass were never more than five minutes before she resumed, leaving her with an average total of a thousand signs of the cross at one Sunday Mass of about two hours. After Mass, she would continue until she reached home, where the greater part of her domestic chores was still interspaced with the same style of prayer. By the end of an ordinary day, she practically had a total of about 5.000 signs of the cross in her treasury. An approximate calculation would have left her with something close to 2.000.000 signs of the cross in a year.

Mammy woo Teri never went anywhere far from the village, because she had a discipline not to cross over a bridge. When she came across gutters and shallow rivers, she would bypass the bridge point by going into the gutter or river and coming out on the other side. Since she could not do this with bigger rivers, she stayed in Nkar and prayed until she ran out of energy. For all my teenage days growing up in Nkar, I saw her praying the Sign of the Cross. If we give her the least period of ten years of prayer, she would be a millionaire with some 20.000.000 signs of the cross in stock!

Legend Ten

Wirkom aka Shey Onooh, the Village Musician

From every indication, Wirkom of Roochin was practically the oldest man in the village with more than a hundred celebrations of Christmas by the time his sojourn on earth was over. Popularly known as Shey Onooh, he was a great animator and jester. Those qualities became part of his character, so much that at times he really got confused between reality and phantom, such as the day that rain fell heavily on him and he had nothing to cover himself with; no umbrella, no raincoat, not even a banana leaf to protect himself from the rain. But all the time, he was chewing some leaves profusely and foaming with them at the mouth as the rain beat him mercilessly. Some children begged him to come into shelter with them, but he turned down the invitation saying:

Don't you see what I am chewing? They are special leaves that stop rain from touching you.

When it is raining like this and you chew them, not a drop would touch you. Tell your father to provide a chicken and a calabash of palm wine, and I will initiate all of you into it. And you'll never waste money to buy an umbrella in your life.

And the more he chewed, the harder the rains beat him, yet he continued to profess his faith in the leaves.

Shey Onooh had a flute that he made from an old cassava trunk. The flute was as legendary as the music it produced. He could arrest an occasion with it whenever he showed up, invited or otherwise. After all, who really needed an invitation to a village event? If you could hear the drum or the xylophone, it means you had been invited, and if you had something to take along like food or drink, well, anyone's occasion belonged to everyone. And besides, he had professional dancers like Tamfu Viban, Baa Alidu Wirnkar, and Saafia who just needed to hear that flute and they would dance to style with a religious devotion. The music had special instructions on when and how to turn left and right or stop, for left was right and right was left. If you missed the instructions, you got dismissed from the dancing circle.

The saying was true of Shey Onooh, that it is never wise to offer a handshake to the drummer during a dance. Scripture puts it better: "Do not muzzle an ox while it is treading out the grain" (Dt 25:4). At the peak of his performance, playing the flute and giving orders to the dancers that mesmerized the crowds, everything would come to a halt if someone placed some lumps of corn fufu with slices of meat into Shey Onooh's bag, which he always carried, slung across his chest from his left shoulder. It didn't matter at what level the dancing was: "Haaalt! O mai!" (Halt! It's over). And that was it. He would pocket the flute. Over!

LEGEND ELEVEN

Shey Dama and Baa Lën – troublemakers

Shey Dama and Baa Lën of Nkoomi, also known as Wan Ntoh woo Sènér (the dark prince), were notorious professionals in making people's lives miserable with their merciless tongues. They themselves seemed to have acquired an efficient immunity against insults, for no matter how much they were insulted back, it never really seemed to affect them in any way. The more you insulted them, the more you felt insulted yourself. The best thing to do was to avoid any such encounter with them, for at every time, prevention was better than any cure. As wisdom teaches, never chase a madman for your clothes if you are naked, for he will only run to the marketplace and expose you as the real madman.

Baa Lën's style was to normally start by saying derogatory things about himself, and people would start leaving the drinking place straightaway because they knew what was coming next–someone else.

Yes, I know that I am the only dark-skinned prince of Nkar. And so what? Are dark people not created by God? I also know what I did in Shehri's bar. Yes, I did it on my trousers. Yes. But Shehri is my sister, because she is a princess, and I am a prince of the same palace. Some people don't even have a place where they can do what I did.

Once he hit that jogger against himself, the immunity was tuned, and he could then say anything against anyone with a straight face, and the victim would have nothing to say again. That was the bridge to cross over and attack others:

Look at Nya'ang here, with a belly as flat as a lizard's. Can your stomach even produce a little air? Even if it did, no fly would waste time to check for anything. Have you ever seen electric light? Come to my place and see, even during the day, I will put the electric lights on for you to look, so that at night you can think about it.

On his own part, Shey Dama could reach extremes that even the pen of a scribe would feel ashamed and embarrassed to write down. He insulted even those who did good to him. If someone took pity on him and bought him a drink, he would repay the person threefold with insults, which were sometimes big. Those who knew him, therefore, avoided buying him a drink. But it came to pass on one very hot day that Shey Da, as he was commonly known, came into a palm wine bar hoping for a kind drink, and nobody gave him any, for obvious reasons. He sat so dejectedly, until Tume felt sorry for him and decided to bell the cat by offering him a litre of palm wine. Never was a man so happy with a gift as was Shey Dama that day. Instead of addressing Tume by his full name, he endeared him as Tüüm:

> You see, Tüüm, many people don't believe in Nkar that I pray. You know why? Because, I don't pray for myself. I never pray for myself. When I kneel, join my hands, and look up to heaven, it is your name that I offer to the Almighty. It is you

that I pray for. It is always you, and it will always be you, Tüüm.

Finding his language palatable, Shey Joe decided to add another litre of palm wine. Instead of addressing gratitude directly to Shey Joe, Shey Dama turned but to Tüüm again:

> Tüüm, let me tell you one thing. As you grow older, you will learn, that to say something is not the same thing as to do it. Do you know why I say so? Because there are precisely two of you in Nkar that I pray for – you and Shey Joe. Only the two of you; no one else.

At that point, the decorum and propriety that had reigned for the entire period of Shey Dama's visit disappeared through the window in one moment, as someone he didn't like came in and made the mistake of asking if he could share his drink with him. Shey Dama abandoned the drinks and opened his bazooka mouth on the victim:

Don't you know that I am the god of Nkar? You ask to share in my drink. Instead, I will bless you. I will bless you with poverty and misery. Let money and prosperity be your eternal enemies. Let them run away from you as darkness runs from light. When money sees you, let it run for its dear life, crying that you are coming, so that prosperity and wealth will pack their things and hide away from you. If you put something down to sell at the market, let no one buy it, and if you offer it for free, let no one receive. When you plant something in the ground, let its roots grow upwards to the sky, and if they grow downwards, let a rock come up to meet them. I have blessed you for ever and ever.

People believed in the village that if you met with Shey Dama as the first person to set eyes on in the morning, you could just as well return home, for you were sure to have a bad day.

LEGEND TWELVE

John Tani was frustrated by school children.

There are some groups of people in life that one should really avoid confronting or making them enemies. At all times, they need to be friends. These include school children. They constitute the younger version of Shey Dama and Baa Lën with a major difference in that, if you are nice to them, they will be *Yours truly*, but if you try to play mischief on them, they will outsmart you. Most of the time, their sense of humour abides in incongruity, and they can have great fun of you while hurting and victimizing you as an object of entertainment. They behave like bees; the more you fight them, the more they sting you.

Yaa Vita was a permanent victim of the children of St. Mary's School Nkar. Also known as Yaa Kilon, because she was always threatening that any child she would lay hands on, the parents will have to pay one million francs to settle the case. She had no child of her own in the school but would never miss the

Parents Teachers Association Meeting where she always spoke on only one point: "Use *kasingu* on them. Whip them!" It was understandable, for she had a big farm near the school with fruits and other tempting farm products that a prudent person wouldn't plant near a village school with seven hundred pupils, some of whom came from distances as long as five kilometres, sometimes with nothing to eat during recess time.

The most frustrated of the school children's victim was John Tani whose departure from Nkar was in part or whole the contribution of the children. In those days, there was a popular song whose wordings the children had adjusted to fit in John Tani's name. And it was not nice to hear. They sang and danced "John Tani" all over the village, beginning very early at school. It was almost the school anthem. Even perpetual latecomers started being among the earliest comers to school so as not to miss singing and dancing "John Tani." And that, they did, when the old man would be returning from his palm bush shortly before classes began. As soon as he appeared, the children would arrange themselves in rows, holding on to each other's shoulders in the same manner of display as is done during burials. If you didn't know they were singing and dancing about "John Tani," you could mistake it for a burial, but it was John Tani, old enough to be their great grandfather.

John Tani ee! John Tani eeeeh!
Eeeeh eeeeee John Tani eeeeh!

The verses were more offensive and went something like: "It isn't good to die in misery like John Tani. How can one die suffering like John Tani?" And the dancers would resound the chorus while John Tani pulled past to his home like a military tanker heavily loaded with explosives. That would be it for the day, while the students dispersed into the classrooms to wait for the following day.

Then one day, the tanker exploded, and John Tani gave chase after the children, meaning to catch one and set a disciplinary example on him or her. The children had not expected such a treat. They quickly turned the dancing into the old touch-and-run-game called *Kwahkilar*. This game used to happen mostly after doctrine classes in the evening, when a group of children from different quarters would begin the touch-and-run game to see which quarter would end with the touch. That would be considered that Kwah-kilar has caught you, and no one ever wanted that legendary touch to end with him or her. There were rules such as, you could run and stand on a stone, and nobody would touch you again, or harvest a coffee leaf, or squat down, etc. But there was one type of Kwahkilar known as *Kilehkpuyuv*. This was for the strong, as its only rule was no retreat, no surrender. Some children used to really run and cry, for to avoid being touched, you only had to run; no standing on a stone, or picking of a coffee leave, or squatting. Quarters teamed up and could race across the village right into the night. I had a classmate, Isaac Banye, who could never allow Kwahkilar to stay the night with him. Even late in the night, while you were sitting and warming yourself in your mother's kitchen, you could expect Banye to make an intrusion any time if the last touch had remained with him. Even if you were sleeping in bed, he would not sleep until he was relieved of it with: "M lar ne wo" ("I've touched you"), and before you realized what had happened, he was gone.

Some class four kids became the daredevils with John Tani, provoking him in song and dance with the resilience of Banye. They could come as close as three meters of reach to John Tani. They were aware they were teasing a wounded lion. On that day, John Tani put down his palm wine containers and chased one of the class four kids until classes started. It wasn't more fun, and the boy started to cry as he and John Tani covered kilometres in no time, tearing through coffee farms and reappearing on the school yard, round the school field, round the church, no retreat no surrender. Eventually, the boy made it back to school and dived into the classroom. John Tani marked the classroom very well and went straight to report the matter to the headmaster. He pointed to class four, assuring the headmaster that if he saw the boy, he would be able to identify him. The headmaster asked him to come with him to class four. On seeing the headmaster, there was immediate silence. Then the class prefect tapped the bench in the customary manner for all to rise and greet the HM. They had hardly completed "Good morning, Sir" when John Tani's head appeared through the door, and all hell broke loose. The greeting was abandoned, and "John Tani" took over:

> John Tani eee! John Tani eeeee
> Eeeeh eeeeee John Tani eeeee!
>
> John Tani eee! John Tani eeee!
> Eeeeh eeeee John Tani eeeee!

It was like a spell on the children. The headmaster and John Tani stood helpless and speechless. Then the headmaster turned sympathetically to John Tani and said, "Pa, you have seen the state of things. Go home. I will stay behind and punish them, and we will make sure they stop menacing you." As John Tani walked down the big veranda, the rest of the classes caught the echoes and the entire school became culprit with the eccentric chorus, beating benches and singing "John Tani." Never was the name of one man so sung in a village as was John Tani's. Even birds of the air seemed to have caught up with the chant. And John Tani went home and packed out of the village. And Jesus said: "Offer the wicked no resistance" (Mt 5:1).

LEGEND THIRTEEN

Shuufokavir,
the Man whose Mouth was in the Armpit

Among the legendary myths of Nkar is that of a man said to have appeared in Ntoh Nkar with a mouth located but in the armpit. They called him Njeyih.[11] He ate nothing, drank nothing, and said nothing. With time, the children of the palace came to be placed in his charge as a babysitter when the adults went out to work in the fields during the day. His task comprised serving the children with their lunch at noontime. That went on with no event until an alarm was raised by the children who said that the man was having lunch with them every day when the rest of the people were in the farm and that he could talk through a mouth in the armpit. This was un-

---

[11] In April 1993, I had a conversation with Yaa woo Nsam, a princess of Nkar, who was also one of the oldest people in Nkar, and she recalled the name Njeyih, whose meaning she never got.

believable. But the elders also knew that the children would not tell a lie about something like that, let alone children from Nkar. Mouth in the armpit? How could one even exaggerate such a phenomenon?

Accordingly, some of the elders hitched a plan to hide in the surrounding bushes the next time they set out for the fields. On the arranged day, they hid themselves and waited patiently. Then to their surprise and shock, Njeyih spoke audible words from the armpit, split a kola nut and placed it in the armpit and crushed it. Then he started to feed the little children and himself as well. That was when the elders broke out from their hideout and caught him red-handed, inspected him, and behold, a mouth in the armpit!

He then started to sing his sorrows, recounting his plight, while he was being escorted out of the village, and nothing was ever heard of him. Where he went to, no one knew. But no one would dare lay hands on a man with a mouth in the armpit. Who knew if he was a god? The song he sang came to be known as *Kigha'h*, meaning "a marvel" and since then has been considered as a royal dance for the princes and princesses whose flutes and drums only come out when one of theirs dies or for a very high-ranking traditional ruler, recalling the words of the strange man:

> Princes and princesses of Nkar, what should I do?
> The nobles of Nkar palace, what should we do?
> Even blacksmiths and those with jiggers on their
>   feet,
> Like Fai woo Kov, are also pointing fingers at me.

Thereafter, this mysterious man became known by his handicap, as *Shuufokavir*, meaning mouth-in-the-armpit.

LEGEND FOURTEEN

The Devil's Bridge where Two Titans Clashed

Myth and fear can make one a prisoner in his own house. We were not supposed to talk when passing through certain places considered as sacred in the village and were instructed not to look at a certain *Yuwah* tree near River Tsemkan. Not "to look" was a way of speaking, meaning that none of us with mystical powers should ever try to communicate with the spirits that were believed to abide in that tree. The bridge over the river at that point was a big bundle of bamboos tied tightly together and placed across the river with fragile hangers for protectors on each side. Some distance below that bridge was a waterfall called *Shukindzev* that produced greater noise than its real size and volume. Spirits were also believed to reside there. And to make matters worse, the Fon and the traditional priests performed annual sacrifices there, rendering it even more frightful. The entire area of about a square mile from the tree to the bridge and to the waterfall carried an air of mystery and fright. To pass that way at night required someone with *shiliv she Joro* (a brave heart).

A belief arose in the village that the devil was also using that bridge to go to his farm, crossing at very late and very early hours of the day, and if one happened to be crossing over the bridge at any of those moments, one would surely meet with him. Nobody claimed ever meeting with the devil in person on that bridge, but it was strongly believed to be true. Everyone who was cited as having met with the devil was either living too far away for verification or must have died. And that kept the myth alive, which in turn kept people indoors or sent them home early, making sure to cross to safety before the devil-hour. The procedure was that if you met with the devil on the bridge, when you place your foot on one end, he would place his own foot audibly on the other end. This myth grew so fat on fear until one day two elderly Christians had to cross from either side at a very early hour, considered as the devil's crossing time. They reached the bridge at the same time, and it became a clash of the titans. None of them had a lamp or a torchlight of any sort.

There was a pious belief that, if you lashed at the devil with the holy rosary, he would catch into flames. That was what was about to happen that morning, as the man placed his first foot on the bridge and the woman placed hers on the other side. They clearly heard each other's step and took it for the devil's. The session was repeated for some minutes, then each took the decision to cross. With their rosaries raised high, ready to strike, they met at the middle of the bridge, and the battle over the Tsemkan Bridge started. It lasted for a few minutes with each person lashing at the other with the rosary, expecting the flames to explode. It was a fierce battle that could have landed the fighters into the river beneath. Then the man coughed, and the woman recognized him and called him by name. Everyone who attended daily Mass knew that cough and its owner. He, too, recognized her voice and called her by name. And the fight ended. That was how the devil was beaten and sent away from that bridge with rosary lashes.

LEGEND FIFTEEN

The Conversion of Wuber, the Dreaded Thief

The name Wuber became synonymous to theft. Sometimes children would just say, "You are Wu." Now a repentant and visibly happy man, Hubert Wanyu, is one of the most jovial men anyone would like to meet. Known in his days as Wuber, he gave the village a bad reputation outside that made people look on people from Nkar generally as thieves. And at home, in Nkar itself, even today, no one would dare to name his child as Hubert. That is still considered a dangerous name, the name belonging to the most dreaded thief in Nsoland: "Now all glory to God, who is able, through his mighty power at work within us, to accomplish infinitely more than we might ask or think" (Eph 3:20).

On Thursday the 24th of February 2022, I met him in his beautiful compound of Kong in Mvem where he rules as a respected Christian traditional ruler. That afternoon, we spent hours on his past life, digging out how he became a thief, and a dreaded one, for that matter even proverbial, and his encounter with the grace of God that turned him completely round. He strongly believes that theft was the actual Original Sin, and that if you teach a child not to take what does not belong to him, he will keep the rest of the commandments.

"Taachu," Wuber called out, addressing me by the Lamnso word for priest, "look at the story of Adam and Eve very well. They were thieves. Don't mind whatever people think or say was the actual Original Sin. Adam and Eve stole from God's tree. That is all. They were thieves. That was the first sin. And it came from breaking the first commandment:

Thou shall not take what does not belong to you. That is the first commandment of God. To sin is to steal and to steal is to sin. If a child grows up with the habit of stealing, forget it. He is lost, for he will break any of the ten commandments. If there is a sin to be avoided, it is theft. And to repent from sinning means to repent from stealing. Once someone re-pents from stealing, you can trust the person with anything. That is why Jesus had to die with thieves to save sinners, right? Maabu Nkar!"

He interwove the story of his life so beautifully with some historical events of Nkar that made me wonder if this was really Wuber, for when we were growing up in Nkar and went to various secondary schools in Kumbo, it sufficed to say you were from Nkar to be termed a thief—all because of Wuber. Even in Nkar itself, although the rest of his family members were not thieves, they nevertheless suffered the stigma of bias and prejudice from Wuber who was considered the greatest thief in the entire land of Nso. He could have won a national award if it came to competition. His quarter of Taaron also came to be stigmatized with suspicion and was referred to as

Antavi Dzen (Overside the place of the strong). His neighbour Baa Matu used to heavily load his canon and come out at midnight, shouting insults at Wuber's family: "From father to mother, brothers and sisters, children, all thieves! Thieves!" And he would fire the canon and go back to sleep while the echoes resounded down the valley and throughout Kov Nkar. Baa Matu had his own issues also. He had an ancient bicycle that he had bought since the days that Southern Cameroon was still a territory under Nigeria. If he rode the bicycle to the market in Jakiri, then on coming back he would carry the bicycle. He had a scrupulous sense of corrective justice: "Since you carried me to Jakiri, it is my turn now to carry you back to Nkar."

Wuber gained such notorious fame as a thief, that everywhere a burglary took place, news would circulate that it was Wuber, even when he hadn't the slightest idea about the incident. As the years went by, he became more and more of a victim to his name than a culprit of his deeds. He cheated death many times in most unimaginable circumstances. In the neighbouring village of Ngomrin, some six kilometres from his home, he was thrown over a high cliff and rocks of enormous sizes hauled after him and yet, when the people went to verify the following morning, not a sign of Wuber was seen. After such operations, he usually would disappear to other towns like Foumban or to the faraway big city of Douala and only return to the village after he had caused another atrocity there. People said he had an Indian ring which, when swallowed could make him disappear and appear at will. It was not surprising therefore when he reappeared in the village after some months following the narrow escape from Ngomrin. He was in good shape.

Born in 1939, Wuber was known among his pals as Grand. Events leading to his conversion and repentance from a terror-striking bandit to an ardent Catholic Christian and a responsible traditional ruler are memorable. He gives many thanks to God for Fr. Michael de Rooy, Fr. John Njingti, and the Fon of Kiluun whom he considers as the visible and tangible agents of God's grace in his conversion. When he made his private confession to the priest, it was necessary, for pastoral and social reasons, that he be given a public penance for the people to accept him as a converted man.

Unfortunately, when Wuber was undergoing his public penance in the first stage of conversion under Fr. Michael de Rooy in the early nineteen seventies, a major burglary occurred in Nkar that left the village speechless. Nobody could believe that such an operation could take place in the village and Wuber would be innocent of it. Invaluable items were ferried away from the church and from the Fon's palace. Some of the items stolen from the palace were classified items that could not be seen by just anybody, male or female, as they fell under the category of "unseen" sacred elements of the land. The pain that the burglary inflicted on the pride of the village was considered deep and beyond pardon.

Wuber had been given the penance of sounding the church bell every day for the *Angelus* at midday for three months so that everyone could pray for him and with him. The rumours were spontaneous that he had abused the penance by using it as a spying occasion on the priests and the church's treasures only to bring his friends from Foumban to operate.

Wuber was therefore suspect number one. And the forces of law and order came all the way from Bamenda, the provincial headquarters, to arrest him. Wuber pleaded innocent, but no one could believe him. Maybe if they had not accused him forthrightly, he would have been of greater help in tracking down the thieves than the forces of law and order. But prophets are not accepted home, and Wuber could not be the exception.

The Fon met with the highest traditional council in the state house known as the *Lav Wong* (State House) and after concerting with the members and the ancestors, decreed the use of the traditional ululation (Shiree), which is a ritual carried out by all the people of Nkar to fight against malicious occurrences on the land. It is the voice of the people that is believed to resound the voice of God, not only mystically, but is the loudest sound one can ever hear in Nkar and is executed only when the evil is of a great magnitude. It is rarely used, and the decision to use it can be compared to that of the United States to use the Atomic Bomb on Japan to end the Second World War. Other cases in recent time that have warranted

its use include the fight against the caterpillar infes-
tation known as *ntem-ntem* that attacked crops like
locusts and threatened the tribe with famine. It is reputed that the evil people who had brought these de-
structive insects into the village had also closed the
mouths of the birds from eating them, but the day the
ritual was carried out, the mouths of the birds of the
sky were opened and they descended on the insects
and by the following day, not even one caterpillar
could be seen even for medicinal use. The land was
cleansed of them.

Then, there was the case of scabies and the case
of abortion. From infants at their mothers' breasts to
the oldest persons on the land, everyone comes out
on a designated day with ashes and *kilun* (wild berries). They smash the *kilun* underfoot at every road
junction, raise the ululation, and blow the wood ash
into the air with the incantation: "Wu dua kilun! Wu
dua kibveh" (Let him (the culprit) turn into wild
berry! Let him turn into wood ash). When this ritual
takes place, the whole village lies quiet in a frightful
silence. Prior to the exercises, there is a preliminary
rite known as *Ntamir* (blockage), which is done at

designated areas considered as major entries or exits of Nkar land. This rite blocks any form of evil from entering the land or from exiting so that it can be dealt with accordingly.

The burglary that happened at the time when Wuber was doing his penance was of such gravity that it deserved all the rites and rituals against evil, from tradition to religion. And after all was said and done, it was declared that none of the stolen items had gone out of Nkar land. But where they had been hidden, no one knew. The church and the palace had been badly hit. The men organized themselves and kept watch at night at every area under suspicion while the women and children were instructed to keep their eyes open during the day and their mouths shut. The village was on high alert. At night, men stayed in the bushes armed with Dane guns, spears, and matchets. This went on for days, until one night, at about one o'clock, a pickup truck drove into the village almost without sound and pulled up in front of one Mfuh house in Taaron, Wuber's quarter. The driver seemed to have been tipped by a sixth sense as he suddenly reversed, and before anyone could take a move, had wheeled the vehicle round, and headed at top speed towards Jakiri. A fast runner took to his heels to the church, and acting on agreed signals, woke up Fr. Fred Ten Horn.

Rev. Fr. Sifrinus Germardus Ten Horn, MHM, served in Nkar alongside two other Dutch priests. Popularly known as Fr. Fred, he was a proactive man by nature. He carried anything that needed to be transported in his Volkswagen car, which he used to carry stones for the construction of the Domestic Science block popularly known as Domi. No doubt, he was the first responder who braved and toured the lifeless villages around Lake Nyos after it exploded on August 21, 1986, and killed approximately 2.000 people. Tern Horn could brave things. And that was what he did that morning in Nkar when he got up from his sleep, took his famous Volkswagen, and gave chase after the said pickup. When he reached the intersection at Jakiri and was wondering if the vehicle had taken the road to Bamenda or to Foumban, his instincts directed him to the Foumban road, which was soon confirmed right when he saw the broken barrier bellow the old church building.

As he descended the Kileibah Hill, leading to Ber, he saw the lights of the pickup disappearing at the tail end of the hill, and he was convinced it was the pickup of the thieves. Fr. Ten Horn could run a car, and that night, he ran his Volkswagen. But this was a matter of life or death for the driver ahead who ran for dear life with all that his pickup could give, as he was sure there was an angry hound after him. No one ever knew what would have happened either to Fr. Ten Horn or to the pickup and its driver or occupants, had Fr. Ten Horn caught up with them. The pickup barely managed to enter Foumban before Fr. Ten Horn lost sight of it as it disappeared into acquainted quarters. Fr. Ten Horn took some moments of rest in the silent streets of Foumban that looked so guilty and ashamed in the early hours from hiding a thief. Then he turned his car and returned to base at top speed and was there on time for the six o'clock Mass where his sermon comprised the narration of the ordeal. Everyone in the village believed he must have been armed with a gun, for a Whiteman would not expose himself that far in chasing thieves alone in the night if he was not well-armed.

While Fr. Ten Horn was chasing the pickup, the people decided to investigate the Mfuh house that was now suspected to be the haven for the stolen things, and lo and behold! Everything that was missing was neatly stacked up in the attic. The pickup was coming for pick up and missed being caught by a hair's breadth. While the men were drinking palm wine in the Mfuh house and planning how to safeguard and retrieve the stolen goods, they were all the time hidden over their heads in the attic. The first person who climbed unto the attic and surveyed the spectacle, climbed down shaking his head with disbelief saying, "If there is anyone here who does not *see* everything, he should not climb up there." Everyone understood and gave way for some high-ranking traditional rulers who were among the people present and who happened to be one of those people in the village that "sees" everything. He came and went up the attic and saw and confirmed.

A few days later, Wuber was brought up from Bamenda to Ntoh Nkar for a general interrogation by the village. Everyone was summoned to the palace. It was a spectacle. They all believed he was behind the theft; that is, everyone except one person - the Fon.

Wuber: Taachu, I am sure you were still very young and little to have come to see Wuber in the palace that day.

Fr. Eugen: Certainly, I was still very little in class one, but we heard everything that happened in the palace since we were not allowed to go there.

Wuber: That day, the Fon and Nwerong Nkar summoned everyone to come to the palace and hear me give testimony about my involvement and participation in that operation. I was handcuffed and brought from Bamenda in the back of a military land rover with bodyguards. Yes, Taachu. I had bodyguards. I was treated as a very important thief. Few criminals in Nso have enjoyed the VIP treatment I had, though in handcuffs. When we arrived at the palace, I was amazed at the population I saw there–waiting for me. I jumped down from the back of the land rover like a monkey. Hahahaha. I was not worried at all because deep in my heart, I knew I was innocent of that theft, but who could believe, since I was Wuber. I had been guilty at other times, but not this one. I was so relaxed that it offended Pa Amadou Fonkpu and Fai Wan Shilun so much that they saluted the Fon in the traditional manner and then approached the Commandant who brought me and told him to leave me with them and go. They told him I was their child and that they would know how to handle me. What they meant was that they would kill me. I was already judged and condemned as far as they were concerned. The Commandant understood and told them he had to ensure my security and that not a hair on my head would be touched. They were disappointed. I worsened matters when I pulled out a cigarette from my chest pocket and lit it. There was an uproar that I had disrespected the Fon enough. Although in handcuffs, I was functioning very well with my personal issues and almost enjoying the show.

Then the interrogation started. I answered every question from the Fon and the people, and every time I asserted my innocence, that I knew nothing about the theft and that I knew no one who was involved or who organized it. And I meant it. But that didn't mean that if I wanted to know I wouldn't have known, right? The Gospel says that the truth will set you free. You see that old late Fon of Nkar? He was both a truthful and a wise man. It was his witness to the truth and to wisdom that defended and saved me from the Nkar people that day. The Fon had the last word on that day and threw the entire situation into confusion with his wisdom. Unfortunately, he had many corrupt notables around him.

The Fon told the people that fourteen witnesses had been to Bamenda to testify against me and none of them had said anything that matched with the other, except that I was a thief and had stolen in the village and elsewhere before, and therefore was guilty. That was their testimony against me. Was that enough witnessing against an accused person over a particular crime? He asked them, but very few people answered. Everyone thought this was a golden opportunity to do away with the notorious me, guilty or not guilty, and the Fon was depriving them of it by seemingly defending me. But the Fon was not just going to let his people judge a son of his land unjustly even if he did not trust me himself. He pointed out to his people and all those present, making it clear that he was not speaking for the priests, that the things stolen from the palace could not have been accessed without someone who knew where they were. Those things were both sacred and secret. If Wuber stole them, as they said, he would like to know from Wuber how he got to know where they were. They said that Wuber spied on everything while doing his penance; was Wuber doing his penance in the church or in the palace? They should answer him. Or was Wuber a spirit? No one answered, probably because the spirits were there themselves. I sat before the Fon like the woman caught in adultery. Only that my own case was different. I was not caught in the act of stealing. I was accused. Similar to what happened in the Bible, some people started to leave when the Fon fired those questions at them. I took notice of everything.

Taachu, there is a saying in Nso, that when justice does not favour the lawmaker, the case disappears in the walls (Nsah kõh taala yi nen lai vibu'h). I don't want to say too much about that. But following the

Fon's observations, my case was adjoined to history. The Magistrate brought me back to Up Station Bamenda, and the following day, he gave me transport and told me, "Case dismissed and cancelled. Go home." I came up home, but thought to myself that if I alighted from the car at Taaron, news would circulate that I had gone to Bamenda and escaped from jail as usual. Luckily for me, it was Ntangrin, Jakiri market day. So, I decided to come out at Jakiri, had a couple of drinks there and made sure I was well seen by those from far and near, then I walked home majestically, passed through the Gendarmerie post in Jakiri, before going home. That was the end of the matter, Taachu.

Fr. Eugen: Right to today, many people still believe in Nkar that you had a hand in that burglary, and it still vexes some people who say that you took advantage of your penance to spy on the priests and the church. Can you still defend yourself even now? Even myself, I am also being converted to see you from a different perspective, for I grew up believing that you had a hand in that operation.

Wuber: Taachu, let me tell you one thing? At that time when the theft happened in Nkar, I was already getting so fed up with my previous way of life and there was a growing excitement and desire for God in me. Just as the Fon defended my innocence in the palace, that is the same way God defended my innocence in the church. I strongly believe that we should give to the Fon what belongs to the Fon and give to God what belongs to God. Is that not what you teach? At the time of the incident, I would have been the last man to steal from anyone, let alone from the church. I was enjoying my conversion. I was amazed myself when I started feeling a deep sense of respect for what was not mine. One day, I was moving down towards the road from our home when a large bundle of something fell off a passing taxi from Kumbo to Jakiri. My companion immediately ran to it. It was large, and we were all curious about the contents. When we carefully opened it up, we discovered it was a set of very specially made juju attires for the Kikum dance. My friend was elated.

"We have become rich like this," he said. And I asked him, "How?" "We will sell all of these things for not less than a hundred thousand francs," he said. I told him not one thread was going out of that bundle. He looked at me in utter shock, and I asked him, "When we sell these juju costumes and when they will be used somewhere and people want to know from where they were acquired, and they are traced to us, where will you say you got them from?" He was tongue-tied.

It was not long before the taxi returned, and I gladly handed over the bundle to the happy owner who gave us 500frs. You know the value of 500frs in those days? That was the transport fare from Kumbo to Bamenda. That is the money that brings joy, not stolen money or money acquired from stolen goods.

Fr. Eugen: That was indeed amazing.

Wuber: Yes, it was. And that was how I also treated some fellows who showed up at my house with a big goat asking me to sell it for them. I asked them if they did not know the road to the market. Coincidentally, that day happened to be a Kavi, the Kumbo market day. I told them to take it to the market. Again, this change of attitude in me amazed me also.

Fr. Eugen: The grace of God was beginning its work in you. But tell me, given your experiences with such things, could you not have cleared your innocence better before the Nkar people by helping the authorities find the real thieves? What help did you offer as someone versed with their tactics?

Wuber: Did I know them?

Fr. Eugen: But you earlier hinted that you could know them if you wanted to, right?

Wuber: You are right? But who would have believed that I was not one of them? Because I was accused, I became more absorbed in defending myself than in searching for the real thieves. Besides, the stolen items were already retrieved, which made getting to the thieves even more difficult. And if really the people had used me rightly, instead of accusing me, things could have turned out differently. And Taachu, do you also think I could have remained completely blank about it, thereafter? No way! As I told you already, when the hands of the lawmakers are not clean the case disappears in the walls. The Fon knew better than those who wanted to use me to cover things up.

Fr. Eugen: But it also seems to me that you knew something of what the Fon knew.

Wuber: Hahahahahaha! You sound as wise as that Fon yourself. Do you learn all this in the seminary? I like you, but I am telling you all these things too as a priest, for we are all your children and in need of advice. When you preach in church, tell people to respect what does not belong to them. Stealing is a bad thing, and I will tell you without mincing words what led me into stealing: Bad friends! Bad Friends! Bad friends! *C'est la vérité.* If you make thieves your friends, you will also become a thief. If you move with prostitutes, you are already one! If you don't want to smoke cigarettes, avoid those who smoke cigarettes. Avoid even the smoke. Bad friends! Bad friends! Nobody is perfect, but there are bad people. Bad friends! Tell the children to avoid bad friends, and they will grow up well. Bad friends! Nothing corrupts a young person more than bad company. I was not born a bad person, but I got into bad company and learned their lessons. Tell the children to avoid bad friends. I was not a thief at heart, but bad friends led me into it. I take every responsibility for my bad actions, but when a team wins a match, do people not give the glory to the coach who was not even playing? Viola!

Fr. Eugen: Thank you very much for this message. I will deliver it as much as possible. You promised to tell me the story of your conversion. Now, I know how you got into the thief-thing. How did you get out of it, so much, that you now fight against it with all your heart?

Wuber: You see Fr. Michael de Rooy? When I say Michael de Rooy, I say that as care of Chia John

Shang who reported me to him, that I was a thief of the highest order, perhaps beyond redemption. Born and bred as a Catholic, I was not practicing the faith at all. I was not going to church, and I was not receiving the sacraments, and I was cohabiting with my wife. Fr. Michael de Rooy came after me like a kite after a chicken. Then, do you see Fr. John Njingti? When I say John Njingti, I say that as care of Fr. Patrick Nchuwa. I will tell you the roles they played in my conversion. And lastly, the Fon of Kiluun? The late Fon of Kiluun. These are the three pillars of my conversion: Michael de Rooy, John Njingti, and the Fon of Kiluun. They are my holy people. May Saint Fr. Michael de Rooy, Saint Fr. John Njingti, and Saint Fon of Kiluun pray for me.

Fr. Eugen: Amen. It's amazing that all these people you have mentioned have been called from this world.

Wuber: That is why I say they should pray for me.

Fr. Eugen: Amen!

Wuber: I was sitting in my kitchen one day, when I heard a cough that didn't sound like a Black man's cough. It was soon followed by a knock at the door. To my greatest surprise, it was Chia John Shang, my neighbour, closely followed by Fr. Michael de Rooy. I was roasting some plantains, and my kitchen was as dirty as myself, for I had just returned from the farm. So, I did not know whether to offer them a seat or to stand up. Thank God, Fr. Michael understood my predicament and chose to stand. He pulled up and adjusted his big trousers over his big belly and confronted me straightaway with a big voice:

"You, Mr. Hubert? You be Christian pikin, but you no de come for church, you no de come for sacrament, you no want for marry for church, and you no de mark book. Whatti?"

Fr. Eugen: That must have been very embarrassing to you, having visitors greeting you with a series of accusations.

Wuber: And a White Big Father for that matter. Anyway, I was used to being accused, falsely or

rightly. This was more of an accusation from Fr. De
Rooy than a verification. And I turned to Chia John
Shang and asked him in the dialect if this Whiteman
had been told all these things or it was White witchcraft that he had used to know all those things about
me. I knew of course that Chia John Shang had done
his homework as the head catechist. So, I simply responded to the two men of God, that I had heard and
would start coming to church. And I meant it. Their
coming was God-timed. I was beginning to yearn for
God and needed someone to facilitate the process. I
needed a sort of invitation, and that was just when
they came. And I responded by returning their visit.
I just started going to church. Sometimes, when I sat
on the pew, only few brave men would sit on it again.
Hahahahaha! *Satan done come church*! Unfortunately, it was too sweet to last. Satan got jealous of me
and sent the gang of thieves that broke into the
church and into the palace. I became prime suspect
and victim. Taachu! Ali Baba and the forty thieves!
Did you learn of that story in school? Arabian Nights
Entertainments. Hahahahaha! Taachu, I had a rough
time with tough lessons. Let me tell you something?

As a priest, never join the crowd to hate anybody. Never do it. Everyone can hate somebody, even a bad person, but not the priest. If the priest hates someone, because that person is bad, tell me where that person will go to? Of course, you understand this is different from the young people who make friends with bad people. Yours is a mission to change bad people into good ones, without being an accomplice in their evil. When I returned from Bamenda after being released by the Magistrate, nobody wanted to see me in the village again. I was hated by everyone. So, I had to leave the village again for my own safety.

Fr. Eugen: That must have been very painful to you, especially when you knew you were innocent.

Wuber: Yes, it was. But I am not sure I really cared much, for, at least, I deserved some punishment. Even if I was not guilty of that theft, I was guilty of others, right? So, I was not completely an innocent man. For me, it was just another adventure, although a painful one. Eventually, I came back again to the village and went to Fr. Michael de Rooy who proved more of a friend to me than an accuser. His friendship converted me more than anything. During my first visit to him, before the incident, he had even given me money, enough to buy a packet of cigarettes. That was an incredible gift in the seventies, and that, to a man whom nobody wanted to see in the village. I owe him so much. I remember how he pulled out a large pod of kola nuts from the bin basket beneath his office table and gave it to me to break open. When I did, to our surprise, it produced twelve nuts. When I told him that there were twelve nuts, he beamed up with a smile and asked me if I understood the message of the twelve kola nuts? I said yes.

"Aha! You savy! You savy! E mean say you go be na apostle for Jesus Christ."

That was how Fr. Michael pulled me to church by befriending me. As the process for my mending continued, he even went as far as providing for whatever was pending to complete the marriage requirements with my wife's family for us to be able to get married in church. His concern for me was also proof that he did not believe I had stolen from the church and was more interested in saving my soul than saving the stolen things. It felt like a dream. It was so good. I felt loved without any conditions. Before I could wake up from that dream, my marriage banns were already in their third and last publication in church, and the date of marriage was arranged and announced, still to everyone's disbelief, that Wuber was getting married in church. Then I started to wonder and to doubt it myself. Was it real that I was getting married in church? The devil was not sleeping, and one week to the marriage day, I escaped to Douala. Hahahaha!

Fr. Eugen: Seriously? How funny!

Wuber: Yes, Taachu. I escaped. I was not ready either spiritually or materially. I could not see myself getting married in church as a poor man. I was used to being called Grand, and how could Grand get married like an ant? I escaped to Douala and was there for months. When I eventually returned to the village, the noise about my marriage had died down. I came back quietly like a prodigal boy, but this time, I avoided Nkar and spent most of my time around Jakiri area. Then one day, *Wanmabuh* from Kiluun was returning from a death celebration somewhere and had a stopover in Jakiri. I was never a juju fan, but someone convinced me to come along with him to salute the Wanmabuh. I went along and entered the juju resting place. Since I had just returned from the city in Douala, I had some money, and I lavished it on Wanmabuh by providing a crate of beer. The Wanmabuh people were so happy and expressed their appreciation with *hai hai hai hai!* A few days after, I received a cordial summons from the Wanmabuh that I should report to its house at Kiluun on the day its members usually meet once a week. The issue was that, since I had seen the juju, I had better just come and complete my initiation as a full member known as *Ngang Mambuh*. I didn't object. On that day, I went over there in grand style with more beer that was received with even more *hai hai hai hai hai*!

Normally, when the initiation of a new member takes place for any of the jujus in the palace, they must bring part of the goodies to the Fon who is the overall owner of all the jujus in the palace. When they brought the Fon's portion of what I had brought for my initiation, it was a bit more than usual. That made the Fon curious about the new member. Those who had taken the Fon's things to him were hesitant to call the name of the new member, for obvious reasons. When the Fon insisted that he would not receive the items unless they brought the new member for him to see personally, they had to comply, and I was summoned. I was also reluctant to appear before the Fon. We were all right with our fears. As soon as I was ushered into the Fon's presence and he looked up and recognized me as Wuber, he cried and carried hands on his head lamenting: "Yebei! Yebei! Yebei! Ngang Mambuh rey ki dze Wuber a?" (Was that new member Wuber?)

Taachu, I stood there and got frozen. Goose pimples developed on me, and the saliva in my mouth went hot and dry. I have never felt so embarrassed in my life. I asked myself if this was all about me, a thief. Had I become this bad, that at being introduced to the Fon, I could not be praised for some good thing that I had done, but my name and presence were causing but fear and rejection? That was my final moment of decision to quit stealing for life. I made a silent decision before the Fon of Kiluun that I will never again take what does not belong to me, even a pin. It was the moment of grace executed by the Fon of Kiluun who could not hide his disappointment in me. Fr. Michael planted, the Fon of Kiluun watered, and let me tell you how Fr. John Njingti handed me over to Jesus.

Fr. Eugen: All ears!

Wuber: When the Fon recovered from his shock, he asked me to come closer to him. And that was how he kept me closer to himself until his death. He told me that nothing is ever rejected in the Fon's palace, and as such, he could not reject me. I should just be a good man. And I resolved to be a good man. When we went back to Mabuh's house, I was received once more with *hai hai hai hai hai*, especially as the Fon sent me back with a big cock and a calabash of palm wine.

Fr. Eugen: Your story resembles that of St. Paul.

Wuber: I am coming. I told you earlier, that as a priest you must also be like the Fon, father of the good and the bad. When I returned home from Kiluun to Nkar, I did not waste time going back to church. Unfortunately, Fr. Michael de Rooy had gone on leave, and the priest that received me was Fr. Patrick Nchuwa, who was assisting Fr. De Rooy. I told him that I wanted to give something significant to the church. He seemed not to know about my earlier escape from marriage in the church and advised me to get a set of vestments in the four colours that priests use for the celebration of Holy Mass. I did not know that an ordinary person like me could buy such holy items for the Church, and I was so excited. I could have sold everything to buy those vestments. I was more excited to get the vestments than to get married in church. I placed an order in Douala as directed. Then my special almsgiving was announced in church, and there was a jeer, not a cheer, which was understandable, for this was a man whose marriage bans had been announced in church previously, and he escaped. How could anyone trust anything from him?

When I told my sisters that the vestments the priest was going to use at the celebration of my Thanksgiving Mass would be from me, nobody believed. They promised to hear me on that again. I was seeking to prove in every way possible, even to my family, that I was a different man, but circumstances were not favouring me, so much that right on the eve of my special Thanksgiving Mass, the vestments had not arrived from Douala. It was already Mass time when the package arrived and met me in the house, waiting. I took off for the church at top speed and entered the Church when it was already offertory time, and I danced like a mad man to the altar and went straight and gave the package to Fr. Nchuwa. That Nkambe boy did something I will never forget. He untied the package and took out the green chasuble, removed the one he was wearing and put on the new one I had brought, right there on the altar. That was like accepting me, right? The church went wild with singing and music.

Fr. Eugen: Fr. Paddy needs to hear this. Does he remember this incident. He is now retired and lives in

Nkar. You need to find time and visit him. He also contributed very much to my priestly vocation. So, we all owe him gratitude and praise.

Wuber: Taachu, it gives great joy in one's heart when we appreciate and bless those who plant and water God's grace in our lives. You see, the Church was helping me to regain some good name and popularity in the village. People were warming up to me and starting to treat me with some sincere respect and confidence and not flattering me with "Grand! Grand!" when they needed a drink but dreaded me in their hearts. Having good friends is the best thing that can happen in your life. I was being accepted, but it still felt so strange to me, and the more I was trusted in the village, the more I started to distrust and not to accept myself. And typical of me, I escaped to Douala again, and this time, stayed there for a longer period. But the hand of God was already on me, and I knew I had to return home to properly return to God. Taachu! "Home be home!" If you cannot find God at home, you will not find him anywhere.

Fr. Eugen: I like the way you put it. Godliness begins at home. In ordinary language, charity begins at home.

Wuber: By the time I came back home, I met Fr. John Njingti. He was ready for me, and I was ready for him. A short man like me, we made a match; not afraid of anything. He did not give me a breathing space until I ascended to the altar with my wife, and he blessed us as husband and wife. This is my wedding ring. Fr. Njingti was the one that nailed me to the Church. As you can see, I am a child of many hands.

Fr. Eugen: Don't you think you and family and friends should organise a day of thanksgiving in commemoration of these your three pillars? That will give you occasion to pray for them, celebrate them, and tell people about them. It's a wonderful story that needs to be celebrated. It will also be an occasion to celebrate, not just your conversion, but to celebrate you. You are a man to be celebrated, hoping that as an old man now and a family head, you will not escape to Douala again.

Wuber: Hahahaha! Don't mention that. I've been thinking about all these things. It's just this war that has spoiled everything. Both the government soldiers and the separatist fighters have come to my compound here many times to harass me, asking me to give them the medicine I have. They seemed scared of fighting each other and have turned now but on us the weak unarmed ordinary people. All these kidnappings, arrests, torture, burning of people's homes, and killings, what do they really solve? I tell them, if they are sick, I can harvest leaves and barks of trees and make concoctions that can treat many illnesses and diseases, but anything out of that, I tell them, they should go elsewhere. I am for peace, and no one should try to put anything on me.

Fr. Eugen: Surely, they know you and might have heard something about your past because when we were growing up and hearing about you and your exploits, there were stories that you had a certain ring from India, which you could swallow and disappear and reappear at will.

Wuber: Lies! I trust in God's power. God only! Even as a thief, I just realize now how much I trusted and relied on God. Taachu, do you know that God also protect thieves, not for stealing, but he also loves them, and I believe he will judge them accordingly and punish the wicked ones. The guardian angels sometimes protect thieves from being killed. If those who do evil things only knew how much God loves them, they would stop. But you know sometimes we tell those lies about rings and herbs until we begin to believe in them ourselves, and that is how many get to die. Even when we used to have some of those things and thought they could help, I grew up to see how deceptive those things are. Magic. Lies. If I am alive today, it can only be thanks to God. Don't mind the noise people make about rings and leaves. Why do they die again when the rings are still there in India and the leaves are growing in the forest?

Fr. Eugen: You really cheated death many times. God must have been preparing you for this sweet part of your life. It's like the good wine at the marriage in Cana, that came but later.

Wuber: Indeed. God keeps good things for those who wait. But let me also tell you one thing, let it not look like God loves me more than other people who do or did similar bad things like me. Many are dead. Why? Is it because God loved them less? No. It is because of their hands. There was blood in them. All this noise I am making about innocence, what innocence can a thief talk about? Taachu, I can only speak as a repentant man for the simple reason that I was not a thief at heart. I look back and I think that I might even have stolen at times for adventure, adventure with bad friends. Number two reason why I am still alive today is that I never shed blood in all those adventures. I had friends who killed. My hands are clean of blood. God did not allow me shed blood, to take away someone's life for earthly things.

Fr. Eugen: You are indeed a blessed man. How did your friends receive your conversion? Did they not regard you as a sort of traitor and therefore dangerous to them?

Wuber: Where are they? Where are they? Thieves don't live long, Taachu. If you take what does not belong to you, you will not live long. Practically, all of them are dead. Look at me, eighty-three years today and strong. I was born in 1939, the year the Second World War started, right? Hahahahaha! I am as old as the Second World War. Look at my pile of Sunday Newsletters. I have them more than our Parish Priest. During the season of Lent, when we pray the Stations of the Cross, I feel like sleeping in church. That was when thieves were nailed on the cross with Jesus in Jerusalem. I go to church to hear Jesus tell me every day: "You will be with me today in Paradise." Taachu, nothing is sweeter than being forgiven by God.

Fr. Eugen: Did you make any effort to share your new-found joy of conversion with any of your old colleagues?

Wuber: Taachu, *est-ce que tu me demandes?* Where are they? You are not getting me. They are dead. There was one person who used to join our bad groups occasionally for petit jobs when he needed money for *mbanga*. He lived not too far from me. When I started going to church, I invited him, and he laughed at me saying that I was stupid in getting up early in the morning, shivering in the morning cold from River Tsemkan, to go to church, while the priests were sleeping or drinking tea. The worst thing, he said, was that those who went to church gathered their little monies and gave to the priests for their tea and petrol, to drive cars in which they could not even offer one a lift. That was empty talk. He was hit on Jakiri market day by a land rover as he returned, drunk from the market with a piece of fresh meat in his bag on Christmas eve. He never recovered, for all his *Mbanga* sense. Others died in similar circumstances or were outrightly killed during operations. Stealing is not a good thing. If you want a place to develop, it must first and foremost be ridden of thieves. They are very bad people. Thieves.

Fr. Eugen: You are right for Scripture says: "The thief comes only to steal and kill and destroy" (Jn 10:10). Before we close this our conversation, is there something you would like to say or address to the people of Nkar and the rest of the world?

Wuber: Taachu, any parish priest in Nkar who fails in the practical wisdom of cultivating a genuine and lasting relationship with the Fon for the general welfare of the people is a loser. Such would be like the one-time-parish priest in Nkar whose only achievement noted by the Fon after so many years was that he celebrated his Silver Jubilee in Nkar. We expect, and I should say, deserve more from our priests than just celebrating their jubilees. A priest means everything to us in Nkar, Taachu. I say this from experience.

Fr. Eugen: I understand what you mean. But don't you think also that sometimes people, especially the people of Nkar, expect too much from their priests. Why do they think they deserve so much from the Church and from priests in particular?

Wuber: Show me one village in Nso, perhaps in the world even, that has produced as many priests and sisters as Nkar has done.

Fr. Eugen: That should make them humbler, and more generous, and kinder towards priests instead, right?

Wuber: Right! In the same manner, the Fon also stands to lose if he doesn't work hand in hand with the priests of the Church. I have seen things, Taachu. I cannot talk to the Fon as I am talking to you now, because you are also my son and friend. Tell your brother priests to be like the Fon of Kiluun, loving and accepting everyone, good or bad. That is why Jesus gave them that authority to reconcile the world. Let them not judge and condemn bad people like me, but to help them see the light. Then, tell the children, your little brothers and sisters, the young people, to be careful of the types of friends they make. They should avoid bad friends. Bad friends must be avoided like germs, for nothing corrupts a child more than bad company. As the saying goes: "Show me your friends and I'll show you who you are."

Fr. Eugen: Thank you very much for making this point. Wisdom teaches that if you make a point and the point does not make you, you haven't made a point. Thank you very much, Taa woo Kong.

Wuber (Hubert Wanyu) – Fai woo Kong

Conclusion

By Fr. Cornelius Sa'fe Meyeh

It has been said that the history of the world is the biography of great people. This couldn't be truer than in this great work by Fr. Eugen Nkardzedze that has presented the history of Nkar through narrating the stories of some of its significant citizens. Sometimes it is the events that make the people great, and at other times it is the people that make the events great. This account of the myths and legends of Nkar village appeals to me like a village dictionary or encyclopaedia. It is a reference book that embodies the traditional saying, "Seh fo Nkar foo Nkar" (Take from Nkar and give back to Nkar). The successful weaving together of cultural and religious stories in this book has presented a beautiful relationship that one finds common in Nkar between tradition and religion, the Fon's Palace and the Catholic Church, which makes it really difficult not to be Catholic when you are from Nkar.

REFERENCES

Berinyuy, Charles. The Mill Hill Missionaries in Cameroon: 1922-2022. Bamenda: Destiny Prints, 2022.

Chem-Langhëë, Bongfen. "The Transfer of Power and Authority in Nto' Ngkar," Nso' and Its Neighbours: Readings in Social History. Edited by B. Chem-Langhëë and V.G. Fanso, assisted by M. Coheen and E. M. Chilver (from printed manuscripts of 1987).

John Paul II. "Address to the Aborigines and Torres Strait Islanders in Blatherskite Park" 1986 during his pilgrimage in Australia in 1986.

Jumbam, Kenjo. The White Man of God. London: Heinemann Educational Books Inc., 1980.

Jumbam, Martin. From the Highlands of Nkar to the World. Denver, Colorado: Spears Books, 2022.

Miller, R.C. The Language Gap and God: Religious Language and Christian Education. Boston: Pilgrim Press, 1979.

Verdzekov, Paul. "Sixtieth Anniversary of the Priestly Ordination of Father Aloysius Balon Wankuy." Unpublished, 1 July 2009. Ntasin-Bamenda.

ABOUT THE AUTHOR

Eugen Nkardzedze, PhD, is a Cameroonian priest from Nkar Village in the Diocese of Kumbo, but presently serving as *fidei donum* in the Diocese of Beaumont in Southeastern Texas. He is also author of *The Spirituality of Humor and Laughter: Why Good Things Happen To Bad People* and his recent bestseller *Keep the Basket away from the Casket: Seven Indictments against the Collection of Mass Offerings in Church.*

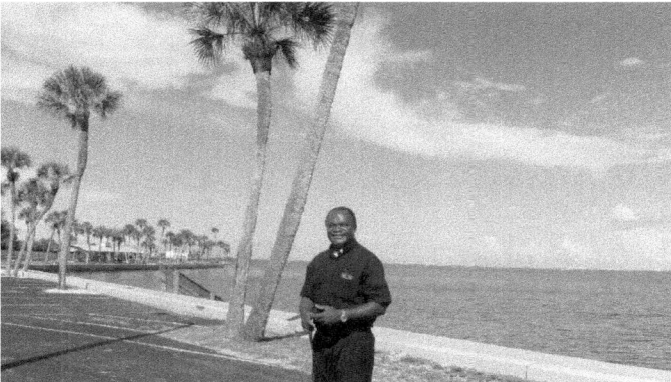

www.ingramcontent.com/pod-product-compliance
Lightning Source LLC
Chambersburg PA
CBHW052005090426
42741CB00008B/1564